旅する根付

高円宮妃現代根付コレクション

写真・文 高円宮妃久子

Have Netsuke *Will Travel*

H.I.H. Princess Takamado Contemporary Netsuke Collection

Photography & Text by H.I.H. Princess Hisako of Takamado

KODANSHA

凡例

・本書における記述は、作品名、作者名、素材名、
　寸法、テキスト、撮影場所の順にした。
・作品名は、箱書などにある
　作者本人の表記のままとした。
　訳は著者の記述に従った。
・作者名は、日本人は「姓・号」の順に記し、
　ローマ字表記では「号・姓」として号を大文字とした。
　外国人は「名・姓」の順で記し、姓を大文字とした。
・素材は、根付の慣例に従い、
　主な素材の記述にとどめた。
・寸法は、最大寸法のみを記した。

Technical Points

· For each netsuke, we have given the pertinent information
　in this order: Name of the Work, Name of the Artist, Material,
　Dimensions, Essay, and Where the Work Was Photographed.
· For the titles of the works, we have used the titles written on
　the boxes. Otherwise, we have used the English (or Japanese)
　titles provided by H.I.H. Princess Takamado.
· The names of Japanese artists are given in the order of Family
　Name followed by Artistic Name, with the Artistic Name in all
　caps; those of foreign artists, are given in Western order
　(Given Name followed by Family Name),
　with the Family Name in all caps.
· As is the general custom with netsuke, we have listed only the
　main materials used.
· For dimensions, we have listed only the largest measurement.

目次

Contents

はじめに

　海外に住むと自国に対しての知識の乏しさに気づく、とよく申します。私が最初に「根付」に注目したのは英国にいた大学生の頃、大英博物館の展示で出会った時でした。洗練された美しい日本画や蒔絵、お能のような幽玄の世界とまた違う日本人の感性がユーモアたっぷりに、しかし高い完成度で根付の中に表現されていました。小さいのでそれまで見過ごしていたのでしょうが、一旦気づくと不思議と引き付けられ、手元に置きたいと思うようになりました。学生の身には高価な骨董品は論外でしたが、日本で夏休みを過ごしている時に行ったお店に、破損のため売り物にならなかった昭和初期の根付があり、それをお願いして分けていただきました。いまでも根付が制作されていることを知り、少しずつ数を増やしました。

　10年後には宮様も興味をもたれるようになり、根付の蒐集家となられました。宮様が亡くなられた後も、日本の伝統工芸品として、また外国に通じる小さな親善大使として、根付文化を守り続けていこうと思い、少しずつ集めております。

　本書に収めたような根付の撮影を始めたのは、宮様が残してくださったカメラとレンズが傷まないように使い出したのがきっかけです。最初は鳥の写真を主に撮っていたのですが、懇意にしている写真家の方に、自分にしか撮れない写真を心がけることを教えていただき、御所の四季折々の自然や収集してある根付の撮影を勧められました。根付を庭に持ち出してレンズ越しに見ると望遠で見ている鳥の世界とは逆にミクロの世界が接近してきます。小さな虫や草花がバックに写り込み、手のひらに収まる根付も写真の中では大きな存在感を示します。

　大学時代写真部に入りましたが露出計算などは苦手でした。いまだそれは改善しておりませんが、最新のカメラの性能とプロの方の助言に助けられながら、日本国中、そして外国にまで根付をもって行き、苦心して撮った写真ばかりです。それはさながら"旅する根付"のあとを追いかけるカメラマンのような心境でした。ゆっくりとご覧いただき、根付の世界を楽しんでいただけたら幸いです。

In the Beginning

As fate would have it, I came across my first netsuke, not in Japan, but as a student in the U.K. The netsuke on display at the British Museum showed me a humorous yet highly refined quality of the Japanese that was completely different from the exquisite beauty of Japanese painting or lacquerware, or the ethereal spirituality of the world of Noh. Perhaps their size had something to do with my having overlooked them until then, but once they make their presence felt, netsuke knew how to keep my attention. I bought my first netsuke—a slightly damaged piece from before WWII. I have never looked back. My collection gradually increased, mainly with contemporary netsuke. When my late husband saw it, he became an avid collector, too. I still continue to collect netsuke, my excuse being that they are a traditional Japanese art form and merit support as little ambassadors for our country.

This book of photographs results from my having tried to put to use the cameras and lenses left to me by my late husband. A professional photographer friend whose advice I sought suggested that I take pictures of my netsuke in the Akasaka Palace gardens. It was an eye-opener to see the micro-world that surrounded the netsuke when seen through camera lenses. The presence of tiny insects and plants became more evident, and the little netsuke made themselves look very big and important. So, many years on from my photography club days at university, but thanks to the kind advice of professional friends and the wonderful cameras that exist nowadays, we have finally been able to put together this book. The combination of two hobbies has opened up a new world for me, and I thank everyone who was involved in guiding me along this path. Each photograph comes to you with all the warmth I feel for each of my little netsuke. I hope that you will enjoy looking at them.

持ち歩く楽しみ

　本来、根付は脇役であり、ぶら下がっている提げ物が主役です。かつて印籠や煙草入れなどの提げ物と根付は対になるよう題材やモチーフを工夫するなど、粋なお洒落がなされていました。今の時代であれば、根付と提げ物の関係は、携帯ストラップと携帯電話。お洒落として楽しむところも含めて共通しているのではないでしょうか。いつの時代もお洒落は他人に見てもらいたいものです。いつも携帯電話をよく置き忘れる私に長女が「持ち歩かなければ携帯の意味がない」と言ったことがあります。そうであるなら、もともと提げ物用の携帯ストラップだった根付を持ち歩くのは当然のこと。多くの方に私の根付をご覧になっていただく機会と考え、これからも根付と旅を続け、また根付を通して未知の世界へと旅をしていきたいと思っています。

Mobile and Traveling

　Netsuke play a supporting role to the lead role played by inro and tobacco pouches. They were fashion items and much thought went into coordinating the subject matter and design motifs represented. Nowadays, the equivalent relationship is seen, at least in Japan, in mobile telephones and the straps that adorn them. Show and tell is a must, so they are truly "conversation pieces". My eldest daughter once complained, "If you leave your mobile phone in your room, it's not being mobile!" If that is so, then netsuke should be mobile, too, for they adorned objects that went from place to place with the wearer. That gives me a very good excuse to continue traveling with my netsuke, throughout the real world—and sometimes into an imaginary one.

Spring Scents きざし

啓蟄 田中俊晴 河馬の歯 長81mm *Spring Awakening* TOSHIKI Tanaka Hippopotamus tooth L:81mm

共存

小野里三昧

黄楊、象牙　幅44mm

「ハート」型の大宇宙の中に地球、

裏面から見ると、

「心」の文字。

象嵌は、駱駝の骨から珊瑚まで、

生命あるさまざまなもの。

地球は象牙で作られています。

（東京・明治神宮）

Co-existence

ZANMAI Onosato

Boxwood, ivory　W:44mm

A person's heart is all-embracing, like the universe. The character for "heart" (*kokoro*) is carved on the back of this heart-shaped netsuke, in a prayer for peaceful co-existence.

(Meiji Shrine gardens, Tokyo)

寿老 <small>じゅろう</small>

藤田寶山
象牙　幅61mm
鶴を抱いているので寿老人。
鶴に松を合わせて、さらにおめでたく。
冬のやさしい陽射しを浴びた
雪吊り松を背景に撮影しました。
（東京・明治神宮）

Longevity

HOZAN Fujita
Ivory　W:61mm
One of the Seven Lucky Gods,
Jurojin sits with a Japanese
crane, a sign of longevity.
Taken in front of a pine that is
ready for the winter snow.
（Meiji Shrine Gardens, Tokyo）

老婆

田中光幽
象牙　高56mm
夕暮れどきの浜辺を、老婆が歩いています。
今しがた、島から帰って来たのでしょう。
背中の荷物が重そうです。
嫁ヶ島を背景に撮影。
（島根県・宍道湖畔）

Old Woman

KOYU Tanaka
Ivory　H:56mm
An old woman with a lantern walks along
the shore. Perhaps she has returned
from a visit to the island. Taken with the
island of Yomegashima in the background.
(Lake Shinji, Shimane Pref.)

せせらぎ

桑原　仁
鹿角（かづの）　長57mm
残り雪の下からふきのとうが芽を出し、
もうすぐやってくる春を知らせています。
ふきのとうの周りの雪も作品中のもの。
裏面には魚の泳ぐ小川も描かれています。
（島根県出雲市・斐伊川河口）

Spring Stream

JIN Kuwabara
Stag antler L:57mm
The light green of the giant butterbur
(*Petasites japonicus*), a sharp contrast
to the white snow, is a sign of the
awakening of spring. On the reverse side
is depicted a stream with fish.
(Hiikawa Estuary, Izumo City, Shimane Pref.)

福寿草

落合　雅
象牙　径25mm
やわらかい春の陽射しを受けて
福寿草がいち早く黄色い花をつけます。
土中の虫たちも活発に動き始めたようで、
裏面にはかぶと虫の幼虫が隠れています。
（島根県・宍道湖畔）

Adonis

MIYABI Ochiai
Ivory　φ:25mm
The soft spring sunlight shines
on the yellow petals of an adonis
(Adonis amurensis). In the soil,
insects awaken. On the reverse side
is the larva of a beetle.
(By Lake Shinji, Shimane Pref.)

13

豆大福

高木喜峰
象牙、黒檀、黄楊　幅40mm
大福の上には、黒豆に見立てた「福助」が、
側面には、逃げる鬼や豆が描かれ、
節分の豆まきを連想させる豆大福です。
「鬼は外、福は内」
奥のお菓子とこの根付。どちらがおいしそうですか?
(宮城県白石市・宿泊地)

Lucky Cake

KIHO Takagi
Ivory, ebony, boxwood　W:40mm
On top of this *daifuku* cake is
a tiny little "Fukusuke," and on the side is a demon running away from
the Setsubun beans. "Fuku" means good luck. The artist plays with
the words and with the design, but the technical work and rendition is
brilliant. (Shiroishi City, Miyagi Pref.)

鬼遣 おにやらい

鈴木裕貴

象牙　幅42mm

いつも逃げてばかりではなく、豆を打ち返す
鬼がいてもいいのでは、と作られた作品。
思い切って曲げた鉄棒や膨らませた頬に
躍動感があります。

（高円宮邸）

Demon Batter and Bean Ball

YUKI Suzuki

Ivory　W:42mm

Our demons, or *oni*, are supposed to run
away when we throw beans at them at
the beginning of the Chinese New Year.
Well, most run away! Some hit homeruns!

(Residence, Tokyo)

大茶盛 おおちゃもり

宮澤　彩

象牙　高42mm

鎌倉時代から
奈良の西大寺に続く茶儀に
「おおちゃもり」があります。
当日は、火鉢のような大茶碗で
お茶が回されます。
蛙の殿様も
かしこまっていただいています。
（島根県斐川町・出雲キルト美術館）

Big Bowl of Tea

AYA Miyazawa

Ivory　H:42mm

Since the Kamakura Era,
there exists this custom
of the "Oochamori" in
Saidaiji, a temple in
Nara.
People partake of the same
tea from a huge tea bowl.
（Izumo Quilt Museum,
Hikawa Town, Shimane Pref.）

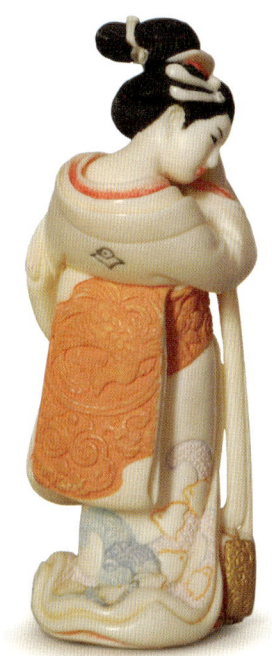

残り香

駒田柳之

象牙　高34mm

三味線と扇を手にたたずむ女性。
「美人を彫らせたら柳之の右に出る者は
いない」といわれ、清楚な表情が美しい。
帯の裏を通す自然の紐通です。

（東京・赤坂御用地内）

Lingering Scent

RYUSHI Komada

Ivory　H:34mm

A young girl, with a classically sculpted
face, stands holding a shamisen and a fan.
Ryushi is an absolute master in his portrayal
of beautiful women. Natural *himotoshi*.

（Akasaka Palace gardens, Tokyo）

東風こち

福山恒山

ココボロ　高59mm

坐禅中は「馬耳東風」のはずですが、
修行不足のせいか、桜の花に心が揺らいで、
眼が動いてしまうのです。
ココボロ材は、中南米に多く産出し、
心材が赤褐色で、黒い縞やまだら模様があり、
サザンアメリカンローズウッドともいいます。

（東京・三笠宮邸）

East Wind

KOZAN Fukuyama

Cocobolo (*Dalbergia retusa*)　H:59mm

This horse sits in the lotus position
and meditates. Still only a novice, his
concentration is broken by the beautiful
cherry blossoms that fall in the spring
breeze. Cocobolo is also called South
American Rosewood.

（Residence of H.I.H. Prince Mikasa, Tokyo）

うらら

小野里三昧
檜（錦帯橋古材）、象牙　径52mm
笹舟に乗って花見をする蛙。
笹舟の下の波頭の裏には桜の花びらも。
50年ぶり架け替えられた岩国市の名橋、
錦帯橋の古材を使っての制作です。
（東京・赤坂御用地内）

Spring Frog

ZANMAI Onosato
Cypress, ivory　φ:52mm
The famous Kintaikyo bridge in
Iwakuni is re-constructed every fifty
years. This netsuke is made from
the old wood. A frog passes under
the bridge in a bamboo-leaf boat,
enjoying the view of the beautiful
cherry blossoms
(Akasaka Palace gardens, Tokyo)

オランダ人

M.バーチ（英国）

河馬の歯、牛角、セイウチの骨　高103mm

頭部、胴体、脚部それぞれに異なる三つの素材の特長を活かしつつ、
付着や埋め込みの技法によって強度を保つように作られています。
なぜか顔の表情が作者自身に似ているのです。

（東京・赤坂御用地内）

The Dutch Wigmaster

Michael BIRCH（GBR）

Hippopotamus tooth, bull horn, walrus bone　H:103mm

Using different materials bonded together in a special way, the
artist depicts an amusing figure of a Dutchman. Despite the
different hairstyle, the face is almost an exact copy of the artist's.
（Akasaka Palace gardens, Tokyo）

こすずめ達

木村　静
黄楊　高39mm
4羽の子雀が桜木のくぼみで
親鳥が運んでくるエサを待っています。
かわいいおねだりの声が聞こえてくるよう。
巣が小さく、つぶされている子雀も。
（東京・赤坂御用地内）

Nest of Sparrows

SHIZUKA Kimura
Boxwood　H:39mm
Four baby sparrows eagerly await the
return of their parents. You can almost
hear them! The nest is getting too small for
them, and one of them ends up a little crushed!
(Akasaka Palace gardens, Tokyo)

フクロウ

S.オシポフ（ウクライナ）
西洋柏槙　幅55mm
ウクライナの寒冷地で、雨風にさらされ
複雑な形に生長したセイヨウビャクシン。
その木目とうねりを巧みに活かして
作者はフクロウを創案しました。
（東京・赤坂御用地内）

Owl

Sergey OSIPOV（UKR）
Juniper　W:55mm
Crimean juniper trees grow slowly in
extremely harsh conditions. The artist
uses the qualities of each juniper to
dictate the design of the final netsuke.
（Akasaka Palace gardens, Tokyo）

ごろにゃん

松宮雲舟
マホガニー　長53mm
作者の愛猫がモデルとのこと。
マホガニーの木肌の美しさと、眼に使われた
鼈甲の色でかわいい表情に。
眼とたんぽぽの色をあわせて撮りました。
（東京・赤坂御用地内）

Purring Cat

UNSHU Matsumiya
Mahogany　L:53mm
The artist's cat was the model. In the way
that cats do, this one lies very flat and has
distinctive yellow eyes. The photograph
was taken with the color in mind.
（Akasaka Palace gardens, Tokyo）

胡瓜きざみ <ruby>きゅうりきざみ</ruby>

宍戸濤雲

鹿角　幅45mm

夜鷹は、その鳴き声が
「キョ、キョ、キョッ」と胡瓜を刻む音に
聞こえることから「胡瓜きざみ」といわれます。
鹿角の根元を活かした夜鷹の母子。
（高円宮邸）

Nesting Nightjar

TOUN Shishido

Stag antler　W:45mm

The nightjar has a voice that sounds like
cucumbers being sliced on a chopping
board—hence the cucumber motif on the
back of the piece. A good use of the stag antler.
(Residence gardens, Tokyo)

酔李白
呑み過ぎですよ 李白先生

田村弦道
象牙　高45mm
李白は酒を讃える数々の詩を残しました。
「月下独酌」などは特に美しい。
（高円宮邸）

A Drop Too Much for Li Po

GENDO Tamura Ivory H:45mm
Famous for his love of wine, the T'ang Dynasty
poet Li Po is said to have drowned trying to
embrace the moon's reflection in a lake. He
left many poems praising wine. "Drinking
Alone by Moonlight" is particularly moving.
(Residence gardens, Tokyo)

小雀

稲田一郎
象牙　高37mm
肩に乗せた雀と手にしている瓜が
素朴な雰囲気を作品全体に醸しだしています。
作者は大正・昭和にわたって活躍した根付師で、
その作風は「一郎根付」といわれて親しまれています。
（東京・赤坂御用地内）

Little Sparrow

ICHIRO Inada
Ivory　H:37mm
Ichiro's works, particularly popular abroad,
were almost all exported after World War II.
From the age of 25（1916）to his passing
at 86, he remained an active carver.
（Akasaka Palace gardens, Tokyo）

声はすれども…夜鷹

宍戸濤雲
アンボイナ　高57mm
アンボイナ材は、赤褐色の縞模様と
粗い質感が独特の雰囲気を醸しだす木。
その特長を活かして制作された夜鷹を
夕暮れ時に木の洞で撮影。
（東京・赤坂御用地内）

Nightjar

TOUN Shishido
Amboyna
(burl of the narra
[*Pterocarpus indicus*] tree)
H:57mm
The distinctive qualities of the
amboyna burl make this an
attractive netsuke. It was already
dusk when I placed it in the
hollow of a tree to photograph it.
(Akasaka Palace gardens, Tokyo)

母子猿

小林仙歩

象牙　高42mm

母子の至福の時を両者の眼が
見えるように撮影するのに苦労しました。
この作者は、紐の結び納まりがいいように
紐通しの片方の穴が大きいのが特徴。

（東京・赤坂御用地内）

Monkey Mother and Young

SENPO Kobayashi

Ivory　H:42mm

It was difficult to judge the exact angle from
which I should try to capture the look of bliss
written on the faces of the mother and child.
Senpo's *himotoshi* are distinctive and easy to use.

(Akasaka Palace grounds, Tokyo)

北の哀歌

和地一風
鹿角　高43mm
絶滅危惧種の島梟<ruby>島梟<rt>しまふくろう</rt></ruby>なので
レッド・データ・ブックの上にいます。
開こうとしているのは
自分のページなのでしょうか。
眼が黄色に輝いているのが象徴的です。
（東京都あきる野市）

Northern Notes

IPPU Wachi
Stag antler　H:43mm
Blakiston's Fish Owl is resident in
northern Asia and is possibly the largest
owl in the world. The artist depicts him
perched on a *Red Data Book*, his claw
holding open the page with his entry.
(Akiruno City, Tokyo)

時の番人

G.ストラディオット（米国）
セイウチの化石　高100mm
鉱物の色が付着した素材を巧みに活かして
時を計る蜥蜴を彫り出しています。
爬虫類や両生類は環境の変化に敏感で、
環境悪化を教えてくれる時の番人です。
（東京・赤坂御用地内）

The Timekeeper

Gregg STRADIOTTO (USA)
Fossil walrus tusk H:100mm
The artist used fossilized material
that is unique in its coloring. Reptiles
and amphibians are sensitive to
environmental changes and may act
as our timekeepers.
(Akasaka Palace gardens, Tokyo)

雀のお宿

針谷絹代（陶作 山本篤）
青磁に蒔絵　径48mm
青磁の蓋を開けると、朱に金蒔絵の別世界が。
作者が初めて磁器に蒔絵を施した根付です。
（東京・赤坂御用地内）

Sparrows in a Bamboo Grove

KINUYO Hariya
(Atsushi Yamamoto : Porcelain)
Lacquer on porcelain　φ:48mm
Inside the calm exterior of the celadon
bamboo grove is a vibrant red lacquer
world of chattering sparrows.
(Akasaka Palace gardens, Tokyo)

子犬

S.オシポフ（ウクライナ）

タグアナッツ　長44mm

元々丸い形をしているタグアナッツは、
根付としてデザインしやすい素材。
その特性が存分に発揮されている作品です。
とくに、眼の作りにこだわりをもっています。

（山形県天童市）

Playful Puppy

Sergey OSIPOV（UKR）

Tagua nut　L:44mm

Tagua nuts are naturally round and shaped
ideally for a netsuke. This puppy has
a mischievous expression that tells us that
he will not lie still for too long.

（Tendo City, Yamagata Pref.）

片恋

松本　鈴
象牙　高39mm
乙女心を猫はわかっているのでしょうか？
夢見る乙女の姿が
上手に表現されています。
作者が初めて作品に着色を施した根付。
（東京・赤坂御用地内）

Dreaming of Love

RIN Matsumoto
Ivory　H:39mm
Perhaps the cat sees into her
thoughts. The artist, using color
to this extent for the first time,
captures the dreamy look of
a young girl in love.
(Akasaka Palace gardens, Tokyo)

草笛

平賀胤寿
象牙　高43mm
春の陽射しのもと、菫咲く野で
草笛を吹く兎を上から撮影。
衣の模様と草模様の浮き彫りが美しい。
草笛用の葉を耳で押さえているのです。
（東京・赤坂御用地内）

Reed Pipe

TANETOSHI Hiraga
Ivory　H:43mm
Photographed from above—almost as
if the camera were the notes that come
from the reed pipe. The robe designs
and the grass are carved in relief.
(Akasaka Palace gardens, Tokyo)

わあい

中西宏明

ガラス、漆　長57mm

ガラスの本体に漆で着色。眼は周りが写り込んで
黒色に見えますが、本来は青色です。
漆のお盆に笹の葉を敷いて撮影。
作者は、ガラスと漆を合わせた作品が得意。
（高円宮邸）

Whee-e-e!

HIROAKI Nakanishi

Lacquer on glass　L:57mm

Because this netsuke is made of glass, it reflects
everything surrounding it and was therefore
difficult to photograph. For example, the eyes are
blue, though they reflect the black of the lacquer.
(Residence, Tokyo)

真夜中のデート

S.オシポフ（ウクライナ）

黒檀　長55mm

素材から得た着想はヘタ付きの豆。
豆が実を結ぶには？
作者は三日月のもとで恋を語らう
2匹の黒猫をあしらいました。
（長野県松本市・松茸山荘）

A Midnight Date

Sergey OSIPOV（UKR）

African blackwood　L:55mm

Making use of the light and dark shading of
the wood, the artist carved a bean pod. It
sets the scene for two loving cats meeting
each other under the moon.
（Matsutake Lodge, Matsumoto City, Nagano Pref.）

のど自慢（40頁左）

高木喜峰
ピンク・アイボリー　高43mm
アメリカグンカンドリの雄は喉を膨らませて
空飛ぶ雌に求愛。喉を自慢するから「のど自慢」。
翼の下に歌本とマイクを挟み、
膨らんだ赤い喉袋には音符が……。

Love Song

KIHO Takagi
Pink ivory（*Berchemia zeyheri*／
Rhamnus zeyheri）　H:43mm
In the Galapagos, one may see males of
two of the largest frigatebirds side by side,
displaying to their females. This is
the Magnificent Frigatebird,
blowing up his throat pouch. He holds
a song book and a microphone.

のどじまん（40頁右）

宍戸濤雲
黒檀　高45mm
オオグンカンドリの特徴は黒い羽根の緑色の艶。
ガラパゴス諸島には両者が生息しているので
その雰囲気が出るように撮影しました。
私の印の扇文様が、足裏に入っています。
（高円宮邸）

Love Song

TOUN Shishido　Ebony　H:45mm
This is the Great Frigatebird with his
distinctive green scapular feathers. This and
the preceding netsuke were carved by different
artists for me on the theme "Singing Birds"
and carry my personal symbol, the "fan."
（Residence gardens, Tokyo）

蛙

M.ウェッブ（英国）
黄楊　幅45mm
蓮の葉に乗る蛙を表現しています。
裏面にはWBとWWWの文字があり、前者は作者、
後者はイギリスの根付収集家、ウイリアム・W・ウィンクフォースの
頭文字。彼の特注の根付が巡り廻って私の手許に。
（東京・赤坂御用地内）

Frog

Michael WEBB（GBR）
Boxwood　W:45mm
The initials WB stand for the carver and
WWW for the great English collector William
W. Winkforth, who originally commissioned this
piece. Eventually, it came into my collection.
（Akasaka Palace gardens, Tokyo）

蛙たち

M.ウェッブ（英国）

黄楊　幅54mm

浮き彫りの手法で繊細に彫られた3匹の蛙。
蛙の下の蓮の葉脈に小さな文字で
「クロプトンにて彫る」と入っています。
蓮の葉の上に置いて撮影。
（高円宮邸）

Frogs

Michael WEBB（GBR）

Boxwood　W:54mm

Three frogs in the Iwami style, with very
detailed carving in relief. Signed ¨Carved
in Cropton¨ with the signature of the
artist, in the Iwami-school tradition.
（Residence gardens, Tokyo）

独りぼっちの森

前田　中

黄楊　高40mm

ニュージーランドの孤島にひっそりと
生息してきた飛べない鸚鵡「カカポ」。
いまやその存在さえも危うい。
独りぼっちの森が、カカポの元気な声で
あふれんことを祈りつつ……。

（東京・赤坂御用地内）

Alone in the Forest

ATARU Maeda

Boxwood　H:40mm

A kakapo is a large, flightless bird
known as an "owl parrot" that inhabits
a remote island in New Zealand. It is
an endangered species. We hope that
he will never be entirely alone.

(Akasaka Palace gardens, Tokyo)

草鹿 くさじし

向田陽佳
象牙　高31mm
鎌倉時代から伝わる弓の的「くさじし」。
鹿のぬいぐるみに星模様を描いた的を
4本の紐で吊るして射る。
やっと紐を解いてくれた作者の優しさに感謝。
（高円宮邸）

Grass Deer Target

YOKA Mukaida
Ivory　H:31mm
A tradition since the Kamakura Period, the
kusajishi is a fabric target in the shape of a deer,
stuffed with grass. The strings have been untied,
and this little deer is enjoying a moment of peace.
（Residence gardens, Tokyo）

垣根の王様

The Hiding King

和地一風
鹿角　幅42mm
鷲の首につかまってどの鳥よりも高く
飛んだミソサザイは王様になれたのも
束の間、みんなに追われて藪の中に。
巣が冠の形をしています。
（高円宮邸）

IPPU Wachi
Stag antler　W:42mm
In an old European tale, the one flying the highest
would be King of the Birds. The wren clings to
the eagle and flies highest, but the others do not
accept him, so now he lives as if in hiding.
（Residence garden, Tokyo）

46

アジサイ賞：追いこみ

河瀬欽水
黄楊　長49mm
蝸牛(かたつむり)の背で蛙が追い込みをかけています。
闘病後、時間をかけて制作した作者からは、
「欽水、最後の根付を」とありましたが、
すっかり元気になられて、現在も活躍中です。
（高円宮邸）

Racing Towards the Finish

KINSUI Kawase
Boxwood　L:49mm
A frog jockey is on the back of a snail for the
Hydrangea Stakes. It is bound to be a slow
ride, but he is not giving up! The artist made
this as he was convalescing from an illness.
(Residence gardens, Tokyo)

ガクアジサイ

中村杢治郎
黄楊　高46mm
ガクアジサイに隠れて
蛇をおそれている蛙。そして、
蛙をおそれているなめくじ。
その頭上には
なめくじをおそれている蛇。
三すくみになっている三者を
根付に。
（高円宮邸）

A Hydrangea Frame

MOKUJIRO Nakamura
Boxwood　H:46mm
Hidden in a hydrangea is
a frog preying on a slug.
But unbeknownst to the
frog, there is a snake
lying in wait for him.
Danger lies round every
corner!
(Residence gardens, Tokyo)

鮑と蛤 <small>あわびとはまぐり</small>

宍戸濤雲

象牙　長44mm

海辺に置いたら、動き出しそうなほどに
精巧に表現されています。
思わず手が出てしまいそう。
熨斗鮑と潮汁の
おめでたい組み合わせの根付。

（高円宮邸）

Abalone and Clam

TOUN Shishido

Ivory　L:44mm

This netsuke is so real that if
we placed it by the sea, it would
probably start moving. An auspicious
combination of abalone and clam.

（Residence, Tokyo）

浅蜊 <small>あさり</small>

村松　朋
象牙　幅51mm
ほんもののアサリと並べて
なじみのお寿司屋さんで撮影。
貝と貝の間に紐を通す自然の紐通しです。
（静岡市清水区）

Mussels

TOMO Muramatsu
Ivory　W:51mm
The owner of a well-known
sushi restaurant allowed me to
photograph this netsuke with
his fresh mussels. The netsuke
mussels are just one size smaller.
(Shimizu Ward, Shizuoka)

小さな美術工芸品

　根付には、帯から何かを下げるという用途に応じた制約があります。それは、丸くて小さく、丈夫で、提げ物を吊るすための紐通しがあるということです。大きくては帯の下から通せませんし、ごろごろしては困ります。帯を痛めるような突起物があっても、壊れやすくても困ります。また、根付は宙に浮いた状態で留まっているので、球体やサイコロのような六面体で、どの角度から見ても美しく仕上がっていなければなりません。手に取ってよく見ると、繊細に木や牙が彫られているだけではなく、部分的に鼈甲や海松、貝の象嵌、金工細工、みごとな蒔絵や細かい彩色が施された根付もあります。この小さな、しかし個性のある、美術工芸品を自分のすぐそばにおいて楽しめるのは実に「夢がある」と自己満足している私です。

Artistic craftsmanship

　Netsuke should be round and small (or in the case of *sashi*-netsuke, flat and long), be durable, and have cord holes, for they must fulfil their function of serving as toggles for holding fast some container. As there are no other restrictions, any of the various types of traditional craftsmanship that exist in Japan, not just wood and ivory sculpture, but tortoiseshell, coral, and shell inlay, different metalwork techniques, and various dyeing and lacquer skills may be used. By collecting netsuke, one is able to enjoy the excitement of keeping close-by, examples of all the wonderful traditional artistic skills and craftmanship, not only of Japan, but of the world.

きらめき

Summer Shades

河童　沢井向円　鹿角　高85mm　**Kappa**—*Water Sprite*　KOEN Sawai　Stag antler　H:85mm

初夏

糟谷一空

黄楊　高59mm

透かし彫りは高度な技術が必要です。

複雑に入り組んだ葉の先に咲く

菖蒲の白い花に向かって小さな蛙が

必死に飛びついています。

（東京・赤坂御用地内）

Early Summer

IKKU Kasuya

Boxwood　H:59mm

This netsuke is delicately carved out,

forming a latticework of leaves. It still

has considerable durability. A little

frog leaps up toward the flowers.

(Akasaka Palace gardens, Tokyo)

鵜飼 うかい

針谷祐之

蒔絵　長41mm

蓋には、羽根を拡げた鵜の姿、内側には、水中を泳ぐ鮎、

底部には、鵜飼の舟と漁火が描かれています。いまは自由に羽根を

伸ばしている鵜も、やがては、鵜匠の元で働く運命にあるのです。

（東京・明治神宮）

Cormorant Fishing

MASAYUKI Hariya

Lacquer *maki-e* L:41mm

This box-shaped netsuke is decorated with
cormorant-fishing motifs. The underside shows
the distinctive torch fire and boat that is used.

(Meiji Shrine gardens, Tokyo)

金魚

佐々木裕子
象牙　高38mm
金魚を広い池で泳がせてやりたい、と思い、
池に連れて行きました。やわらかな線で浮き彫りされた
作品に夕べの光がやさしく注いでいます。
2005年の日本象牙彫刻会新人賞受賞作。
（東京・赤坂御用地内）

Goldfish

HIROKO Sasaki
Ivory　H:38mm
Perhaps this goldfish would like to have
a good swim in the lake. A beautiful time
of day, the sunlight of the late afternoon
casts a gentle light on the netsuke.
(Akasaka Palace gardens, Tokyo)

昇鯉 しょうり

相原　博
鹿角　高54mm
滝昇りに挑んでいる鯉の表情には、まだ
余裕が。勝利を目指す鯉だから「しょうり」。
水のはねる感じが、鹿角の付け根の
素材で上手に表現されています。
（東京・赤坂御用地内）

Leaping Carp

HIROSHI Aihara
Stag antler　H:54mm
The carp swims strongly up the waterfall,
confident that he will make it to the top—and
become a dragon! The artist makes good use
of the shape and rough quality of the antler.
（Akasaka Palace gardens, Tokyo）

カイダコ

S.オシポフ（ウクライナ）

タグアナッツ　幅37mm

タグアナッツで上手にタコの
軟らかい質感を表現しています。
透き通った貝を抱えている
足のうねり具合も印象的です。

（東京・赤坂御用地内）

Argonauta

Sergey OSIPOV（UKR）

Tagua nut　W:37mm

The tagua nut is the perfect medium for
demonstrating the texture of the octopus and the
thinness of the Paper Nautilus（*Argonauta*）shell.
Tagua tends to change color over the years.

（Akasaka Palace gardens, Tokyo）

あおさぎ

森 哲郎
鹿角　高59mm
くちばしに黒蝶貝と珊瑚、眼に海松と
トルマリンを使用したのが特徴。
大きな魚を嬉しそうに眺めている
表情を見せるために、ロー・アングルで。
（東京都日の出町）

Grey Heron

TETSURO Mori
Stag antler　H:59mm
This is unusual subject matter for this artist,
but he makes good use of the natural coloring
of the antler. The photograph had to be from
a low angle to capture the bird's expression.
(Hinode Town, Tokyo)

羽根

針谷祐之
蒔絵　径44mm
いちばん美しい鳥が
王様になると聞いて
ほかの鳥たちの羽根を
身にまとったカラス。
しかし、その羽根を抜かれて
元の黒い姿に戻る、という
イソップ寓話を題材にした作品。
（宮崎市・宿泊地）

Feathers

MASAYUKI Hariya
Lacquer *maki-e*　φ:44mm
From Aesop's *Fables*.
The Raven tries to become
a king by dressing up in
other birds' feathers but
is found out. Inside, you can see
the Raven's own feathers.
(Miyazaki City)

森について考える

宍戸濤雲
ピンク・アイボリー　高38mm
いまや絶滅の危機にある「森の人」
オランウータンが座り込んで考えています。
われわれ人間もかつては森の人でした。
「哲人」と森について考えませんか?
（東京・赤坂御用地内）

Man of the Forest

TOUN Shishido
Pink ivory（*Berchemia zeyheri／
Rhamnus zeyheri*）H:38mm
Orangutan means *Man of the Forest*. Here, he
ponders on the future of his forest, and perhaps,
more philosophically, on our place in the universe!
（Akasaka Palace gardens, Tokyo）

興奮の龍壺 こうふんのるつぼ

野垣内秀也

黄楊　高38mm

これから起き出そうとしているのか。
小さな壺の内には納まらない龍は
まだ眼をつぶったままです。
興奮の前の一瞬の静寂なのでしょうか。

（高円宮邸）

A Barrel of Excitement

HIDEYA Nogaito

Boxwood　H:38mm

An awakened dragon climbs out of
a barrel. Although a professional
carver for many years, this artist is
relatively new to netsuke carving.

(Residence gardens, Tokyo)

なき虫

小野里三昧
黄楊　高43mm
指にけがをした蟬の子が泣いています。
しかし、蟬しぐれのなか
だれも気づいてくれません。
本物の蟬の抜け殻と一緒に撮影。
（高円宮邸）

Cry-Baby Cicada

ZANMAI Onosato
Boxwood　H:43mm
A baby cicada cries because it has cut its
finger, but no one can hear him because the
noise created by his companions is too loud. The
empty shell next to the netsuke is a real one!
(Residence gardens, Tokyo)

草笛

東　声方
象牙
長50mm
人びとの生活に牛が密接に
関わっていた時代の
のどかな雰囲気にあふれています。
（東京・赤坂御用地内）

Reed Pipe

SEIHO Azuma
Ivory　L:50mm
A depiction of a quiet pastoral
scene of days not too long ago
when keeping cattle was part of the
daily life of a farming community.
(Akasaka Palace gardens, Tokyo)

ももんが

伊藤滋女
黄楊　高40mm
作者が飼っているモモンガがモデル。
いつも家の中にばかりいるので、
たまには森で仲間と遊ばせては、と
ブナの森に連れて行ってみました。
（長野県飯山市・斑尾高原）

Flying Squirrel

SHIGEJO Ito
Boxwood　H:40mm
The artist's pet flying squirrel was the
model for this netsuke. It is pictured in
a beautiful beech forest, where it would
be able to move around freely!
(Madarao Highland, Iiyama City, Nagano Pref.)

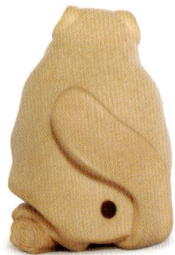

蟬の食事

小林仙歩
象牙　長57mm
くちばしを挿して樹液を吸う蟬の姿。
「蟬の仙歩」といわれた
作者の力量が、羽根や腹部の
繊細な彫りに見て取れます。
（長野県飯山市・斑尾高原）

Feeding Cicada

SENPO Kobayashi　Ivory　L:57mm
This was taken at the height of summer in
a beech forest with many cicadas singing
away in the background. A highly
regarded and popular artist, many
collectors want to own a Senpo cicada!
(Madarao Highland, Iiyama, Nagano Pref.)

虹のかなたへ

福山恒山
アンテロープの角　高185mm
「オズの魔法使い」でドロシーが
飼い犬のトトや家と共に飛ばされる
シーンを表現。アンテロープは、
一対の角をもつウシ科の動物。
細かい彫りのあとで白く着色しています。
差し根付で、紐通しは作品の中ほどに。
（高円宮邸）

Somewhere Over the Rainbow

KOZAN Fukuyama
Antelope horn　H:185mm
A scene from the *Wizard of Oz* in
which a tornado carries Dorothy
away to the start of her adventures.
Some farm animals are also depicted
caught up in the tornado.
(Residence gardens, Tokyo)

龍巻 たつまき

関　凡鳥

象牙　高49mm

わずか数センチの作品に、どのような
物語を盛り込むかが根付師の勝負どころ。
龍巻に龍が巻き込まれるという
発想の奇抜さがおもしろい!

（東京都あきる野市）

Tornado

BONCHO Seki

Ivory　H:49mm

Tornado is "*Tatsu*（dragon）*maki*（roll）"
in Japanese, so the artist depicted
a dragon caught up in a tornado. Of
course, he might also be causing it!

(Akiruno City, Tokyo)

双龍

平賀胤寿

象牙　高34mm

中国で、ある画家が4匹の龍を描き、
瞳を入れた双龍は雷鳴とともに天に飛び立ち、
残る2匹はいまも地上にあるといわれます。
この双龍は、画龍点睛の龍でしょうか。

（高円宮邸）

Dragons Entwined

TANETOSHI Hiraga

Ivory H:34mm

A Chinese artist drew four white dragons in Anraku
Temple without putting in the eyes because he thought
if he did they would fly away. Finally he was persuaded
to do so, whereupon the two with eyes flew off. Could
these be those two white dragons?（Residence）

渇水

小野里三昧

鹿角　高45mm

頭の皿に水がなくなったせいか、
息も絶えだえの河童。
しかし、その愛くるしい表情に、
なぜかホッとさせられます。

（東京・赤坂御用地内）

Water Shortage

ZANMAI Onosato

Stag antler　H:45mm

Kappa are water sprites who must keep their
pates moist. The water shortage that this *kappa*
seems to be suffering is worrying, but his
doleful doggy-like expression makes me smile.

(Akasaka Palace gardens, Tokyo)

河童 かっぱ

森　哲郎
黄楊
高47mm
お酒の入った瓢簞を
片手に、好物のキュウリを
かじっている河童。
足でしっかりと
鰻を捕まえています。
その眼を細めた満足そうな
表情が印象的です。
（東京・赤坂御用地内）

Kappa—*Water Sprite*

TETSURO Mori
Boxwood　H:47mm
This *kappa* is squatting
on an eel, holding a gourd
with sake, and munching
on his favorite food, the
cucumber. His expression
is one of contentment.
(Akasaka Palace gardens, Tokyo)

地鎮プイプイ

中村杢治郎
黄楊　高48mm
度重なる地震に鯰を
戒めに行った河童ですが、
反対に大切な甲羅を
咬み取られてしまいます。
痛くて悔しい河童は、
チチンプイプイ!
地震も痛みも飛んでいけ!
と念じるのです。
（東京・赤坂御用地内）

Give It Back!

MOKUJIRO Nakamura
Boxwood　H:48mm
Angry with the catfish
for causing so many
earthquakes, this *kappa* went
to teach him a lesson.
Now the catfish has taken
his shell, and the *kappa* is
fighting to get it back.
（Akasaka Palace gardens, Tokyo）

暗い夢を食べる獏

M.バーチ（英国）
犀の角　高85mm
150万年前のアケボノゾウの
肩甲骨の化石を背景に。
洞窟壁画のような不思議な空間が、
暗闇で夢を食べ続けてきた
獏のイメージに重なりました。
（東京都あきる野市）

The Baku That Devours Bad Dreams

Michael BIRCH（GBR）
Rhinoceros horn　H:85mm
Photographed in front of the
fossilized shoulder bone of
a stegodon（Matsumoto）, the
netsuke looks as if it is set
deep in an ancient cave.
（Akiruno City, Tokyo）

梟 ふくろう

G.ショー（英国）

海松　高90mm

海松の流紋と
淡い色合いを活かした作品。
梟の足が木と一体化して、
すっくと立つその姿に凛々しさを感じます。
（東京・赤坂御用地内）

Owl

Guy SHAW（GBR）

Umimatsu（black coral）　H:90mm

The artist used the natural flowing
form of the dark coral to create this
hauntingly beautiful figure of an owl.
The eyes are piercing, but warm.
（Akasaka Palace gardens, Tokyo）

山親爺 やまおやじ

針谷祐之
蒔絵　高47mm
梟が巣穴でもの思いにふけっています。
その心象風景が背面に
淡いタッチの金銀蒔絵で描かれています。
巣穴は、桐材に錆漆を施したものです。
（長野県飯山市・斑尾高原）

The Wise Old Owl

MASAYUKI Hariya
Lacquer *maki-e*　H:47mm
The wise old owl looks out of the hollow
and reflects upon what he sees.
On the back is depicted the forest as
he remembers it, or the way that
he would like it to be.
（Madarao Highlands, Iiyama City, Nagano Pref.）

三宝之声 さんぽうのこえ

栗田元正
鹿角　37mm
三宝とは、悟りを開いた人（仏）、その教え（法）、
教えの許で修行する人（僧）のこと。
木葉木菟は鳴き声が「ブッポウソウ」と
聞こえることから、別名「仏法僧」とも。
ちなみに、仏法僧という美しい鳥が別にいます。
紐通しに銅管を挿して、補強しています。
（東京都あきる野市）

Owl of the Three Treasures

MOTOMASA Kurita
Stag antler　H:37mm
The Oriental Scops Owl (*Otus sunia*)
has a call that sounds similar to a word
naming the Three Treasures of Buddhism
"Bupposo" (Buddha-Dharma-Sangha).
(Akiruno City, Tokyo)

レンカクの夢

S.レイト（英国）
黄楊　幅45mm
長い足指で蓮葉の上を歩く珍鳥レンカク。
レンカクが心配そうな顔をして
葉の上の亀を覗き込んでいるのは、
その下にレンカクの卵があるからです。
（東京・赤坂御用地内）

Lotus Dreaming

Susan WRAIGHT（GBR）
Boxwood　W:45mm
The jacana（Jesus bird）peers into the
mischievous eyes of the turtle. She looks
worried, and she should be!
The turtle is sitting on top of her nest!
（Akasaka Palace gardens, Tokyo）

瑞鳥 苦邪食 ずいちょう くじゃく

向田陽佳

黄楊　高131mm

孔雀は毒蛇を食べることから、
古来、「邪を喰う鳥」とされています。
「苦」も「邪」も食べてくれる
瑞鳥のイメージを重ねました。
孔雀の足許には
毒蛇が捕らえられています。

（高円宮邸）

Sacred Peacock

YOKA Mukaida

Boxwood　H:131mm

This beautifully carved peacock
holds a poisonous snake in
its claws. The snake symbolizes
evil. This artist uses no electric
tools in making her netsuke.

(Residence gardens, Tokyo)

隠れ里

和地一風

鹿角 長120mm

好物のキュウリの中が河童の隠れ里？
キュウリの蔓が龍に変わり、その口から
滝が流れ落ちています。滝壺には、
3匹の河童がのどかに暮らしている姿が。
まるで一幅の山水画のような作品です。
（東京・赤坂御用地内）

Hidden Hamlet

IPPU Wachi

Stag antler L:120mm

The imaginary *kappa* love to eat
cucumbers, so inside this one, is a hidden
hamlet. Water flows forth from
a dragon's mouth and 3 female kappa
decorously lounge by the waterfall.

（Akasaka Palace gardens, Tokyo）

四六の蝦蟇 しろくのがま

北澤いずみ

陶器　長34mm

ひび、あかぎれ、しもやけ、キズの妙薬で、
歯の痛みにも効くとされる蝦蟇の油。
前足、後ろ足の指が4本、6本となっています。
蝦蟇の傍らにある油壺とセットで。

（島根県出雲市）

Toad

IZUMI Kitazawa

Ceramics L:34mm

Toad oil was said to work wonders for
many ills and merchants used to sell it
using a special type of rhetoric.
The *ojime* is in the shape of an oil pot.

(Izumo City, Shimane Pref.)

水遊び

阿部裕幸
象牙　高42mm
親鯨が吹く潮の上で遊ぶ子鯨。
とにかくかわいい。
親子の無邪気な姿には
ビー玉がお似合いか、
と特設の海で撮影。
（高円宮邸）

Joyful Whale

YUKO Abe
Ivory　H:42mm
The baby whale laughs as
he is thrown high into the
air on his mother's spray.
Marbles were placed in
the picture to give it
a playful atmosphere.
（Residence, Tokyo）

Tsunami

糟谷一空
黄楊　長50mm
2004年12月26日のスマトラ沖地震による
大津波での大惨禍に想起した作品。
鯰にはおとなしくしていてとの願いを込めました。
沖縄の紅型の布を背景に撮影。
（沖縄県那覇市）

Tsunami
IKKU Kasuya
Boxwood　L:50mm
Created immediately after the
tsunami off the coast of Sumatra
on December 26, 2004. Catfish
are said to cause earthquakes.
（Naha City, Okinawa Pref.）

こんぴら狗 こんぴらいぬ

高木喜峰
黄楊　幅38mm
金毘羅宮に祀られているのは海の神と
航海の神。犬の代参の風習があることから、
柴の子犬を乗せた帆船に。帆の後ろには、
無事に代参を終えた印のお守り札を
入れた箱もあります。（高円宮邸）

Konpira Dog

KIHO Takagi Boxwood W:38mm
Kotohira Shrine, known as Konpira-
san, was a popular center of belief. If
someone was too ill to travel, he might
send a dog, which would be relayed
from person to person to Konpira-san
and back.（Residence）

玉屋ーっ!

阿部裕幸
象牙　高50mm
傘お化け、提灯お化け、一反木綿お化けが
花火見物としゃれこみました。
その音の大きさに驚いて、ひっくり返った
傘お化けの眼には、大輪の花火がくっきりと。
（宮崎市・宿泊地）

Fireworks!

YUKO Abe
Ivory　H:50mm
Ghosts, a part of the Japanese
summer scene, go to watch some
fireworks. The netsuke shows them
quite shocked by all the noise.
（Miyazaki City）

井ヨリ出ズル

前田　中

象牙　高40mm

精巧な細工が施されたからくり根付。
紐が釣瓶縄にもなり、井戸を外すと
蛙とオタマジャクシが「井ヨリ出ズル」。
飾り物としても楽しめる根付です。

（東京・赤坂御用地内）

Frog in the Well

ATARU Maeda

Ivory H:40mm

This is an extremely fine
work with great attention
to detail. It opens to reveal
a bright green frog. The ropes
for the buckets go through
the himotoshi for the moment.

(Akasaka Palace gardens, Tokyo)

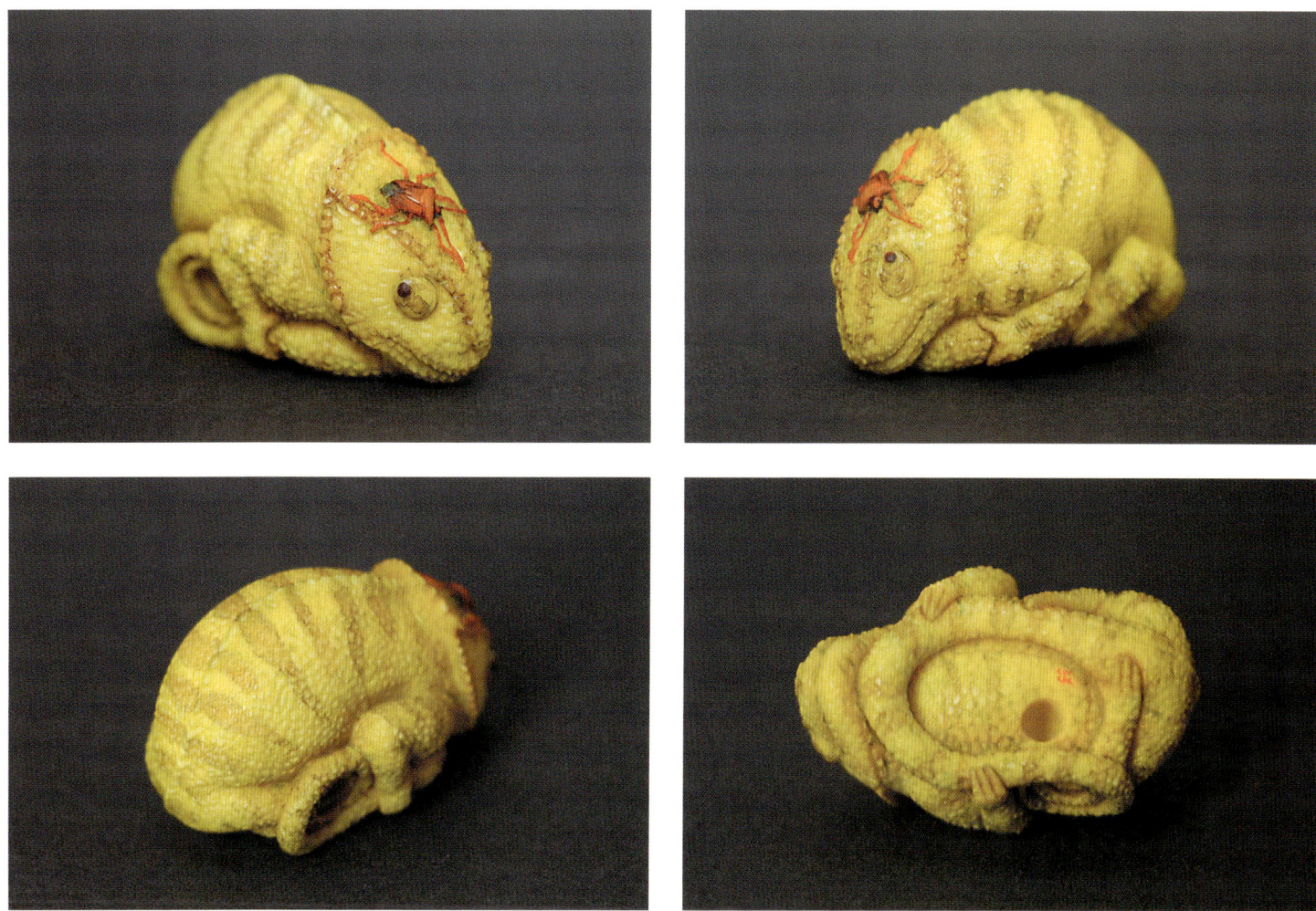

思案

松本　鈴

象牙　幅37mm

象牙を染め、その上に描いたカメレオンの
眼の表情がユーモラスです。

獲れそうで獲れない頭上の餌に思案顔。

腹の脇のくるくる巻いた尾の中が紐通しです。

（東京・赤坂御用地内）

Lost in Thought

RIN Matumoto

Ivory　W:37mm

This green chameleon won the Prince
Takamado Award at the Annual Exhibition
of the Ivory Sculptors' Association. The
tasty looking insect is just out of reach!

(Akasaka Palace gardens, Tokyo)

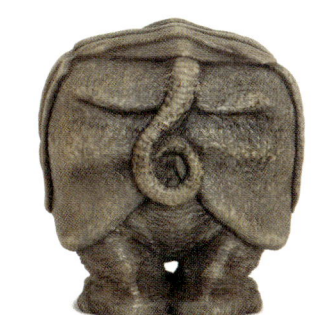

サイコロ

高木喜峰

象牙　高35mm

犀の姿を
四角に作ってサイコロに。
正面の「角」が1、
右側面の「紐通し」が2、
背中の「シワ」が三、
「足の裏」が4、
左側面の「シワ」がV（5）、
後ろ姿の「尻尾」が6です。
相対している面を足すと
「7」になります。
（東京・赤坂御用地内）

The Die Is Cast!

KIHO Takagi

Ivory　H:35mm

This rhinoceros joins the august
company of dice: 1 horn（1）,
himotoshi（2）, folds on back（3）,
legs（4）, fold on side（V=5）, and
a curled tail（6）. As on a real die,
opposing sides add up to 7.
（Akasaka Palace gardens, Tokyo）

沈黙の鳥

向田陽佳
鹿角　高107mm
餌を捕るため、何時間も無声の
直立不動の姿で立ち続ける
アフリカに棲む鳥・ハシビロコウ。
その視線は、捕らえた鯰に。
鯰の眼もまた、ハシビロコウに……。
作者はこの鳥を観察するために、
上野動物園でハシビロコウに
なっていたのでは、と想像します。
（東京・赤坂御用地内）

The Silent Bird

YOKA Mukaida
Stag antler　H:107mm
The African Shoebill is a silent
and strange looking bird. It
stands still for hours, but when it
gets the chance, it will suddenly
spring into action to get its prey.
(Akasaka Palace gardens, Tokyo)

水辺

福山恒山

鹿角　長52mm

生きものたちの楽園であった干潟や沼、池、
浜辺がしだいに少なくなっていますが、
水辺の動物たちは必死で生きています。
いままさに、ヨシゴイが蛙を捕らえた瞬間。

（東京・赤坂御用地内）

By the Shore

KOZAN Fukuyama

Stag antler　L:52mm

This bittern has caught a frog. We are
losing our marshes and swamps and
putting at risk the lives of many creatures
that inhabit such environments.

(Akasaka Palace gardens, Tokyo)

贈り物

S.レイト（英国）
黄楊　高45mm
宮様が残されたたくさんのお言葉。ともに
過ごした貴重な時間。全ての思い出が
宮様からの贈り物。大切な風呂敷包みには
オオマダラチョウが止まっています。
（東京・赤坂御用地内）

The Gift

Susan WRAIGHT（GBR）
Boxwood　H:45mm
The legacy of words and the memories
of times spent together are gifts from
the late Prince. A monarch butterfly
alights on the precious parcel.
（Akasaka Palace gardens, Tokyo）

徳利蜂

梨本寿光

象牙　高39mm

巣の形が徳利に似ているからトックリ蜂。
泥で巣作りに励んでいる蜂の眼や嘴、
頑丈そうな脚には、遭いたくありません。
「義雄」は作者が号を使う以前の名前。

（松江市・宿泊地）

Hornet

JUKO Nashimoto

Ivory H:39mm

A detailed and beautifully balanced carving
of an interesting insect—much safer than
in the wild! An early work by this artist, he
has signed it using his real name, "Yoshio."

(Hotel Gyokusen, Matsue City, Shimane Pref.)

一瞬の輝き

和地一風

猪牙　長116mm

「流星は天狗が空を渡る姿」と
いわれます。烏天狗が流星の
核を捕まえようと手にしていた
羽団扇を放してしまいました。
その団扇が足下に落ちています。
一瞬の輝きを得たいがためには、
だれしも大切にしてきたものを
失うのかもしれません。

（高円宮邸）

A Moment of Brilliance

IPPU Wachi

Boar tusk　L:116mm

The imaginary large-nosed
tengu live in the mountain
forests. Some local tales
say that a shooting star is
a tengu traveling. Also,
because shooting stars
make dreams come true,
the karasu-tengu tries to
grab a star and drops his
fan instead. The message
is that we might lose
something important while
trying to achieve a moment
of brilliance.

（Residence grounds, Tokyo）

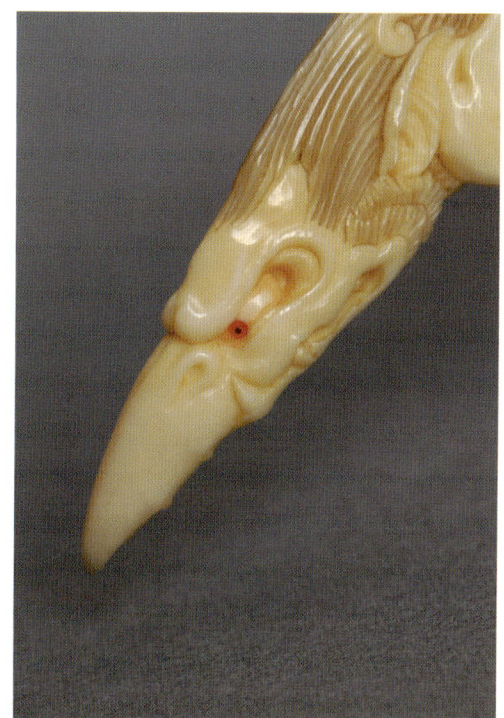

作家の思いを楽しむ

　根付は、あらゆる角度から見ることのできる極小の面に、既存の物語や象徴的な主題を表現していくところに作家としての技量が現れます。どの根付も共通しているのは、制約された形と寸法のなかにスケール感や動きを表現していることです。そのため、自然に見せながらもかなりデフォルメしています。8頭身であるべきものを5頭身、5頭身であるべきものを3頭身に、刀や笛、三味線など長いものを体に添って湾曲させるなどの工夫が凝らされています。また、どこか「えっ?!」「まあっ!」と立ち止まらせる「ひねり」は根付のいのち。作品を見て思わず微笑んでしまうようなら、作家からすると「大成功!!」といったところでしょう。

Netsuke Charm

　When worn, most netsuke are visible 360 degrees. Skill is needed in arranging stories and symbolic themes on a surface that is tiny and yet open to being viewed from all angles. Admired for their charm and delicately detailed work, netsuke convey a sense of scale and movement despite their limited size. Proportions and shapes are changed in order to achieve this, but a good netsuke will still look totally natural. Many collectors also seek some kind of "twist" in the netsuke — something that makes them stop and look. The artists would consider it a great success if huge grins and smiles broke out on the faces of those who saw or held their work.

Autumn Echoes

しのぶる

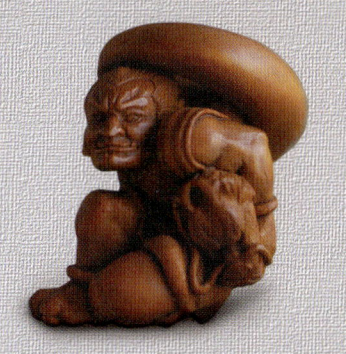

竜巻　鈴木裕貴　黄楊　高40mm　Wind Dragon　YUKI Suzuki　Boxwood　H:40mm

牛若丸

増田秀司
象牙(ぞうげ)　高40mm
悲しい運命を背負いながら
旅の空を眺める牛若丸。
その旅姿を橋の欄干に
置いて撮影しました。
わずか40mmの作品とは
思えないほど
大きく見えるのが
根付の魅力でしょうか。
左手のたもとの隙間が
自然の紐通しです。
（東京・赤坂御用地内）

Ushiwaka-maru

HIDEJI Masuda
Ivory　H:40mm
Dressed for travel,
Ushiwakamaru looks up
at the skies.
Remembering his
encounter with Benkei
on the Gojo bridge,
this netsuke was
photographed on the
parapet of a bridge
in the Akasaka
Palace gardens.
Natural *himotoshi*
in the left sleeve.
（Akasaka Palace gardens, Tokyo）

とこしえに

福山恒山

鹿角、黒檀、ブライアー　高50mm

カナダ留学時代のアルバム、大好きでいらしたサッカー。
このお蔵には、宮様の思い出をたくさん納めてあります。
屋根に黒檀、アルバムにパイプ材のブライアーを使用。
背景は松本城です。

（長野県松本市）

Forever

KOZAN Fukuyama

Stag antler, ebony, briar H:50mm

Memories of my late husband, symbolized
by a photo album of Canada and a football,
are tidily put away within this storehouse.
Taken in front of Matsumoto Castle.

(Matsumoto City, Nagano Pref.)

斑虎 <ruby>斑虎<rt>はんこ</rt></ruby>

平賀胤寿
マホガニー、象牙 長44mm
虎の腰にはとんぼが一匹。
眼と歯には象牙、とんぼには蝶貝を使用。
まだら虎にふさわしい場所かどうか、
斑尾高原で撮影してみました。
（長野県飯山市・斑尾高原スキー場）

Spotted Tiger

TANETOSHI Hiraga
Mahogany, ivory L:44mm
A dragonfly rests on the back of a spotted tiger.
When these prize skins were first imported, it
was thought that the spotted leopards and striped
tigers were male and female of the same species.
(Madarao Highland Ski Resort, Iiyama City, Nagano Pref.)

和

和地一風
黄楊
幅41mm
3匹の兎が耳で円陣を組んでいます。
その向こうではママさんバレーの輪が。
輪は、「和」を生み出します。
(山形県天童市・山形県総合体育館)

Harmony

IPPU Wachi Boxwood W:41mm
These rabbits huddle together in a sign of peace
and harmony. In the background, the women in
this recreational volleyball tournament also go
into huddles before the match.
(Main Arena, Yamagata Prefectural Sports Park,
Tendo City, Yamagata Pref.)

セロム

佐々木明美
黄楊　長49mm
黄楊を彫り上げた
観葉植物セロムは、
葉脈や葉の表面などに
瑞々しさを感じます。
でも、枯葉の上に置くと、
落ち葉にも見えませんか。
（東京・赤坂御用地内）

Philodendron

AKEMI Sasaki
Boxwood　L:49mm
This boxwood netsuke,
depicting the fresh young
leaves of a philodendron,
looks quite natural
among the fallen autumn
leaves, because of the
boxwood coloring.
(Akasaka Palace gardens, Tokyo)

栗

二代目・良舟
象牙　幅61mm
栗とドングリの上では
てんとう虫も
動き回っています。
本物の栗をピカピカに
磨いて混ぜてみました。
見分けられますでしょうか?
（高円宮邸）

Chestnuts

RYOSHU II

Ivory　W:61mm

A basketful of chestnuts
and a ladybird!
Ryoshu II was famous
for his realistic
rendition of chestnuts.
Can you tell the
difference between
the real chestnuts
and the netsuke?
(Residence, Tokyo)

穴掘り名人

福山恒山
鹿角　径54mm
ミミズをくわえて
土中から出てきたもぐら。
つぶらな瞳が
まぶしそうです。
土の中では
蟻も巣作りに一所懸命。
鹿角の付根の質感が
活かされています。
（東京・赤坂御用地内）

Mole in the Hole

KOZAN Fukuyama
Stag antler　φ:54mm
A mole with a big worm,
puts up his furry hand
to block the sunlight.
The underside shows
an ant at work.
Pictured on a real molehill
（of which we have
quite a few!）
（Akasaka Palace gardens, Tokyo）

秋惜しむ

福山恒山
琥珀　長42mm
北海道の高山地帯に棲むナキウサギは、
秋に葉や茎、実などの保存食を蓄えます。
琥珀は、硬くて欠けやすい素材なので
毛彫りなどの細工には高度な技術が必要。
（東京・赤坂御用地内）

Preparing for Winter

KOZAN Fukuyama
Amber　L:42mm
Our pika（rock rabbits）live in Hokkaido.
This one is rushing from one storing
place to another with food for the winter.
Detailed carving using a difficult material.
（Akasaka Palace gardens, Tokyo）

晚秋

小野里三昧
檜（錦帯橋古材）　幅51mm
山口県岩国市の錦帯橋は、春は桜、
秋は紅葉の名所です。
天然記念物の白蛇と紅葉の「紅白」で、
縁起の良い根付です。
（東京・赤坂御用地内）

Late Autumn

ZANMAI Onosato
Cypress　W:51mm
Kintaikyo, one of Japan's most picturesque
bridges, is famous for its spring cherry
blossoms and autumnal leaves. The white
snake is highly valued as being auspicious.
(Akasaka Palace gardens, Tokyo)

狐の嫁入り

松本 鈴
象牙 幅34mm
綿帽子に白無垢の花嫁は、
耳と尻尾がまだ見えています?!
心配そうに寄り添う子狐。
だまし通せるのでしょうか。
（北海道利尻島）

The Fox-Bride

RIN Matsumoto
Ivory W:34mm
Illustrating a saying we have in Japan, this
bride is actually a fox. The photograph was
taken in the very north of Japan, where
there is a wild population of Ezo red foxes.
(Rishiri Island, Hokkaido)

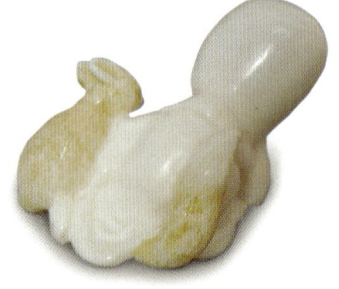

福鳥

佐田　澄
象牙、鼈甲　幅50mm
象牙に鼈甲の象嵌で色模様をつけた
かわいらしい福鳥です。
空に羽ばたこうとする口元が印象的。
羽根裏の象嵌は違う色になっています。
（東京・赤坂御用地内）

Bird of Happiness

SUMI Sata
Ivory, tortoiseshell　W:50mm
Unusual for this artist, who normally keeps
her netsuke pure white, she has rendered
a lot of inlay work. The determined mouth
(or is it a beak?) always makes me laugh.
(Akasaka Palace gardens, Tokyo)

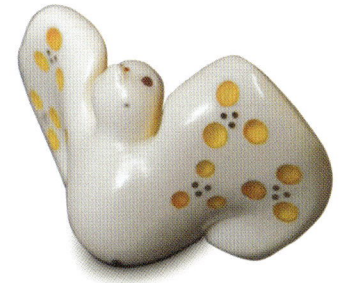

能楽面

平賀明玉斎
象牙　幅33mm
面が逆さまに写り込むように、
黒い漆板の上に置いて撮影しました。
実像と虚像とが合致して、
一つの大きな根付にも見えます。
（兵庫県豊岡市・宿泊地）

Noh and Kyogen Masks
MEIGYOKUSAI Hiraga
Ivory　W:33mm
This artist is the father
of Tanetoshi. By placing
the piece on a lacquer
board, and focusing on
the one overturned mask,
the reflection becomes
part of the netsuke!
(Toyooka City, Hyogo Pref.)

道具

荒巻秀美
象牙　幅40mm
旅役者の道具でしょうか、中身は、
鼓、笛、台本、面など芝居で使うものです。
作者は、いろいろなものを一つに
組み合わせて表現するのを得意としています。
（兵庫県豊岡市・宿泊地）

Stage Props

SHUBI Aramaki
Ivory　W:40mm
Props that belong to some traveling
troupe, put together and carved by
an artist well known for his skills in
this type of group rendition.
(Toyooka City, Hyogo Pref.)

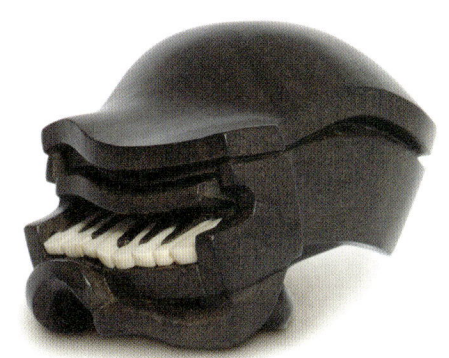

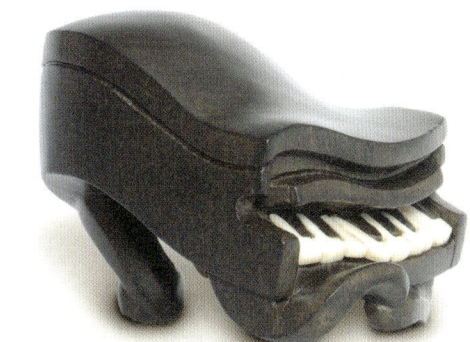

夜想曲

向田陽佳

黒檀、象牙　幅45mm

ドイツのボンにある

ベートーベンの生家。

許可を得て、持参した根付を

ベートーベンが10歳のころ弾いていた

オルガンに置いて撮りました。

（ドイツ・ボン）

Nocturne

YOKA Mukaida

Ebony, ivory　W:45mm

Permission was generously

granted when I asked to

photograph this netsuke piano

on the top of the organ console

played by Beethoven when he

was only ten years old.

(Bonn, Germany)

響

向田陽佳
黄楊、黒檀、水牛の角
高45mm
真っ直ぐであるはずの
バイオリンを
これでもか、というほど
曲げて丸くした根付。
ベートーベンのバイオリンや
譜面を背景に。
（ドイツ・ボン）

Making Music

YOKA Mukaida
Boxwood, ebony, horn
H:45mm
This rounded violin
was also taken in the
house of Beethoven.
On condition
I used no flash,
I was allowed to
photograph this atop
the display of
Beethoven's violin
and music.
(Bonn, Germany)

カーテン・コール

高木喜峰

黄楊

高37mm

殿下の撮られたリスの
写真が印象に残り、
お得意でいらした
チェロ演奏に重ねて作品に。
たくさん拍手をすれば、
カーテン・コールで
戻ってきて下さるでしょうか。

（山梨県・富士山五合目奥庭山荘）

Curtain Call

KIHO Takagi

Boxwood H:37mm

My cello-playing husband

once took a picture of

a ground squirrel in Canada.

After his passing,

Kiho carved this piece

in his memory, hoping

that the Prince world

return for a curtain call.

（Okuniwa Lodge, Mt. Fuji, Yamanashi Pref.）

無限大

高木喜峰
黄楊　幅41mm
宮様の干支は、午。
4回目に廻ってきた
午年に逝去されました。
だから、
メビウスの輪には線が4本。
大きく描かれた
「阿吽の午」の間には
干支の文字が並んでいます。
井伊家の菩提寺で。

（滋賀県彦根市・龍潭寺）

Infinity

KIHO Takagi
Boxwood　W:41mm
The Prince was both
born and passed away
in the Year of the Horse.
One horse has his mouth
open; the other, closed.
The lines indicate
the four cycles of his life.
(Ryotan Temple, Hikone City, Shiga Pref.)

思い出

宮澤宝泉
黄楊
長43mm

Memories

HOSEN Miyazawa
Boxwood
L:43mm

殿下のお好きだったものを、
思い出箱に詰めてあります。
周りに思い出の写真を選んで
寄せ木細工のように施した箱根付。
2006年FIFAワールドカップドイツ大会での
宿泊ホテルの部屋で撮りました。
（ドイツ・デュッセルドルフ）

The artist put memories of
the late Prince both inside and
outside of this box netsuke. I
took it to Germany for the FIFA
2006 World Cup, as he would
have wanted to go.
（Düsseldorf, Germany）

思い出-2

阿部裕幸

象牙　高40mm

日本サッカー協会名誉総裁でいらした宮様は、
毎年国体で地元サッカー協会との
親善試合に参加されていました。
いまも親善試合は続けられています。
2007年、秋田国体のグラウンドに根付を持参。
ボール裏面の時計が指している時刻は、
宮様が逝去された
2002年11月21日の「22時52分」。
（秋田県にかほ市・仁賀保運動公園）

Memories-2

YUKO Abe

Ivory H:40mm

The late Prince was the Honorary
President of the Japan Football
Association and each year he enjoyed
a friendly match with the local JFA
officials during the National Sports
Meet. I asked for the event to continue,
as he would have wanted it that way.
This netsuke shows the time at 22:52,
the time he passed away on November
21, 2002. The netsuke came and watched
the match with me at the 2007 Sports
Meet in Akita.

(Nikaho City, Akita Pref.)

不動明王

大下香征

水晶に蒔絵　高43mm

不動明王を動物で表わすと龍、
物ならば諸刃の剣、
色ならば金または青黒。
背中の炎は
毒をもつ動物を食べる
伝説上の鳥の形に。

（山梨県・富士山五合目奥庭山荘）

Acala, The God of Fire

KOSEI Oshita

Quartz crystal, *maki-e*

H:43mm

Acala, the God of Fire,
is symbolized by the dragon,
the two-way sword and
the colors gold and dark blue.
The fiery halo behind
him symbolizes a peacock,
which eats poisonous animals.

(Okuniwa Lodge, Mt. Fuji, Yamanashi Pref.)

一家だんらん

針谷絹代

蒔絵　長54mm

雄鶏は美しく、雌鶏はふくよか、
雛たちはまるまるした姿で
愛嬌たっぷりに描かれています。
これぞ輝く、一家だんらんです。
漆の作品には漆が似合うのかな、と
お盆に置いて撮りました。

（松江市・宿泊地）

Happy Family

KINUYO Hariya

Lacquer *maki-e*　L:54mm

Good *maki-e* work showing an elegant
cock, a plump hen, and roly-poly
chicks—a picture-book image of
a happy family of chickens. Pictured on
a lacquer clothes tray.

(Matsue City, Shimane Pref.)

親子河童

河原明秀
黄楊　高39mm
川原で腰を下ろしている親子の河童。
籠に入った子どもを見つめている
親の真剣な眼差し。
どこから来たのか、どこへ向かうのか。
（山形県酒田市・宿泊地）

Mother and Child Kappa

MEISHU Kawahara
Boxwood　H:39mm
A *kappa* mother with a child in
a basket—pictured looking down
a river. Where did they come from
and what are they going to do?
What is the tale they have to tell?
(Sakata City, Yamagata Pref.)

祷

前田　中
鹿角　高90mm
いなごや蛙が枝に刺さっている光景を
見ることがあります。
これを「モズのはやにえ」といい、
「ほかの動物への供物」ともいわれます。
そのことから「いのり」という作品に。
（高円宮邸）

Prayer

ATARU Maeda
Stag antler　H:90mm
Shrikes impale the bodies of insects
and other prey on thorns and
branches. This makes it easier to eat
them and acts as a larder, too. Other
animals also eat these "offerings".
(Residence gardens, Tokyo)

フクロウ

D.マースデン（ニュージーランド）
黄楊　高64mm
夕暮れどき、老樹に作った巣から
狩りに出ようとしているフクロウ。
下方には蝸牛や虫がはい回り、
裏面では、お爺さんが渋い顔をしています。
（東京・赤坂御用地内）

Night Owl

Doug MARSDEN（NZL）
Boxwood　H:64mm
An owl looks out from a hollow in
an old tree. There is a snail and
a worm below. The suspicious
expression of the tree as it peers to
see what is going on is amusing.
(Akasaka Palace gardens, Tokyo)

あやしい怪

和地一風

鹿角　高34mm

妖怪の根付には魔除けの意味があります。大きさの異なる三つの眼は、いろいろな角度からもの事を見られるように。蝶貝の輝きも不思議な雰囲気を出しています。底部にある口は「禍の元」。舌が紐穴になっており、表と裏で「目は口ほどにものを言う」とも。これでもやはり、怪しいかい？（東京・赤坂御用地内）

The Eerie Eye

IPPU Wachi

Stag antler　H:34mm

A very strange priest indeed! He has
a third eye on his head, so that he sees all,
and a huge mouth and tongue underneath.
Sometimes the spoken word brings trouble!
(Akasaka Palace gardens, Tokyo)

三ザル

喜多　淳

黄楊　高38mm

「見ざる、聞かざる、言わざる」の三猿。
チンパンジーの研究で有名な
ジェーン・グドール博士の講演会場で。
このニホンザルは
「チンパンジーのことなど
もう聞きたくない」
と思っていたのかもしれません。
（京都市・京都大学百周年時計台記念館）

Three-in-One Monkey

ATSUSHI Kita

Boxwood　H:38mm

"See no evil, hear no evil,
speak no evil" in one.
This Japanese macaque
refuses to hear any more
about chimpanzees
from Dr. Jane Goodall.
(Kyoto University, Kyoto City)

テーマ根付のこと

　本書に掲載されている作品には、年に一回開催している「根付の夕べ」から生まれたものも含まれています。宮様が始められた集まりで、数人の作家が半年ほど前に出題されたその年のテーマに応じた作品を制作し、披露する会です。当日は、夕食を終えてからが本番。作家は緊張した面持ちで作品をご披露し、目を輝かせて丁寧にご覧になっていた宮様の表情が一転し、嬉しそうな笑顔になられるまで、皆固唾を呑んで待っていたものです。作家の想像力を刺激しながら、創造性をつぶさないようテーマを出すには難しいこと。今は私がその年のテーマを選んでおり、そのようにして生まれた作品には私の印である「扇」を銘の近くに彫ってもらっています。

Annual Themes

　Some of the netsuke that appear in this book are the result of annual "Netsuke Evenings," gatherings that were started by my late husband. Several chosen artists are given a theme about six months ahead of time, and they show their work at the dinner. It was always a tense moment for the artists, as they watched the prince look carefully and excitedly at their work, and a moment of pride for them when his face broke into a huge smile. I continue with the evenings, and the netsuke that are made for me in this way have carved on them my personal symbol, a "fan," in some shape or form.

ぬくもり
Winter Glow

鎌鼬 かまいたち 和田 升 黄楊 高40mm **Kamaitachi** — *Sickle Weasel* NOBORU Wada Boxwood H:40mm

うたたね

桜井一桜
象牙　長46mm
静かな冬の夜。
鉄瓶の鳴る音を聞きながら
つい、うたたねをしています。
チンチン鳴っている音も聞こえてきそう。
つい最近まで見られた光景です。
（松江市・宿泊地）

Catnap

ICHIO Sakurai
Ivory　L:46mm
On a quiet winter's night, the sound of
the kettle with its boiling water can be
very soporific. Not too long ago, this
would have been a common sight in Japan.
(Kasuien Minami, Matsue City, Shimane Pref.)

しーっ!
後藤雅峯
黄楊　高38mm（泥棒）　高25mm（犬）
抜き足! 差し足! 忍び足!
しーっ! 吠えないで。
泥棒と犬とで一対の根付と緒締。
結び紐を外して撮影しました。
（松江市・宿泊地）

Shh!!
GAHO Goto
Boxwood H:38mm（burglar） H:25mm（dog）
A typically dressed burglar is not very
successful when he encounters a dog that
he begs to stop barking. The burglar is the
netsuke and the dog is the *ojime*.
（Matsue City, Shimane Pref.）

鯛焼き

宋戸濤雲

黄楊　幅46mm

薄皮には焼きたての鯛焼きが2尾と
半分？尻尾まで餡が入っています。
お腹からはみ出しそうに
餡が入っていておいしそう。

（宮城県白石市・宿泊地）

Taiyaki—*Bean Cake*

TOUN Shishido

Boxwood　W:46mm

Taiyaki is a kind of Japanese sweet in the
shape of a sea bream—and this one seems to
have lots of sweet bean filling and someone
has obviously been tempted to take a bite.

(Shiraishi City, Miyagi Pref.)

手の内

宍戸濤雲

象牙　長74mm

弓道では、烏賊の甲をすり潰した粉末を
滑り止めとして手の内側につけます。
「手の内につける烏賊の甲」としゃれて、
烏賊の甲に弓、矢、弓懸を収めた作品です。
（高円宮邸）

All in the Hand

TOUN Shishido

Ivory　L:74mm

In *kyudo*, or Japanese archery,
te-no-uchi meaning "in the hand,"
is very important. A ground-up
squid bone may be used to stop
the bow from slipping
in the hand. Here everything is
"in the squid bone"!
(Residence, Tokyo)

都会のヤタガラス

針谷絹代（陶作 山本篤）
青磁に蒔絵　高43mm
いまや都会では巣作りもたいへん。
神武天皇の道案内をしたという
八咫の烏は、
日本サッカー協会のシンボルマークです。
（東京都新宿区・都庁）

Crows in the City

KINUYO Hariya
（ATSUSHI Yamamoto, porcelain）
Lacquer on porcelain　H:43mm
The housing situation in big cities
is not easy for crows, either.
The three-legged crow acted as
a guide for Emperor Jimmu, the
first of our long line of Emperors.
（City Hall, Shinjuku Ward, Tokyo）

愉快な妖精

M.バーチ（英国）

海松、鹿角　高50mm

海松の曲がり具合を
活かして作られた
不思議な妖精です。
鹿の角を嵌め込んだ大きな眼が
愉快な表情を作っています。
旅先での短い休憩時間に
アンティークのランプを
背景に撮った一枚。
（秋田県大仙市）

The Wry Sprite

Michael BIRCH（GBR）

Umimatsu（black coral），
stag antler　H:50mm

The gnarled natural shape
of the material turns into
an impish character when
given huge, expressive eyes!
Photographed during
a break on an official visit.
（Daisen City, Akita Pref.）

時運 じうん

平賀胤寿
マホガニー、象牙、蒔絵　高57mm
中国の諺にある
「時に合えば鼠も虎と化す」。
鼠が手にしている鏡には、
虎の顔が写っています。
虎と化したわが身を見た鼠の心境は、
まさに「天にも昇る心地」でしょうか。
（東京・六本木）

Fate

TANETOSHI Hiraga
Mahogany, ivory, lacquer *maki-e*
H:57mm
A Chinese proverb says,
"When the time comes,
the mouse becomes a tiger."
The reflection in the
mirror shows a tiger,
and stripes show on his body.
So this mouse feels on
top of the world!
(Roppongi Hills, Minato Ward, Tokyo)

蓬萊蒔絵

雲龍庵　北村辰夫
蒔絵　長34mm
中国の霊山「蓬萊山」は、不老不死の地。
蓋には、霊獣四神の一つ「玄武」の顔で、
甲羅に毛の生えた緑毛亀が描かれ、
内部には、蓬萊山に止まる鶴と松竹梅の
吉祥が配されています。（松江市・宿泊地）

Penglai-shan

UNRYUAN Tatsuo Kitamura
Lacquer *maki-e*　L:34mm
Penglai-shan is a sacred mountain.
The lid shows a long-lived turtle,
with a ferocious face, and inside is the
crane, also signifying longevity. A highly
sophisticated and auspicious box! (Matsue City, Shimane Pref.)

8一飛車成 はちいちひしゃなり

藤井安剛

黄楊、漆　高43mm

将棋では、縦（段）を算用数字で、
横（筋）を漢数字で表わします。
最強の駒「飛車」が
敵陣の8一で裏返り
「龍王」と化す瞬間です。
将棋の駒の産地での撮影。

（山形県天童市）

Strong Move

ANGO Fujii

Boxwood　H:43mm

This netsuke depicts the
moment in *shogi*, a kind of
Japanese chess, when the
strongest piece turns into
a dragon king. This photo was
taken in Tendo, known for its
production of *shogi* pieces.

(Tendo City, Yamagata Pref.)

火の鳥

針谷祐之
蒔絵　高37mm
蓋には、微妙な濃淡をつけた炎と、
生まれ出ようとする火の鳥が。
蓋を開けた途端に、炎の中から金色に輝く
火の鳥が飛び立ってきます。
火焔は、けがれを清めるもの。
（島根県斐川町・出雲キルト美術館）

Firebird

MASAYUKI Hariya
Lacquer *maki-e*　H:37mm
Different shades of red
are used to portray the flames.
When the lid is opened,
a beautiful firebird become visible.
This artist is highly skilled
in *maki-e* technique.
(Izumo Quilt Museum, Hikawa Town, Shimane Pref.)

ことぶき

増田秀司
象牙　高60mm
提灯を手に夜道を行く女性。
そこには「ことぶき」の文字が。
京都に唯一残存する武家屋敷が、
2007年、根付館としてめでたく開館。
（京都市・清宗根付館）

Felicitations

HIDEJI Masuda
ivory　H:60mm
This lady looks content with
a lantern marked "Felicitations."
How appropriate, then, to photograph
her at the recently opened Seishu
Netsuke Museum in Kyoto!
（Seishu Netsuke Museum,
Kyoto City, Kyoto Pref.）

雲太 <ruby>うんた</ruby>

藤井孝三
百日紅 <ruby>さるすべり</ruby> 高62mm
発掘された出雲大社の巨大神殿跡が実証した、
「出雲大社が太郎（雲太）、東大寺が二郎（和二）、
平安京大極殿が三郎（京三）」の日本三大建築の順。
大国主命 <ruby>おおくにぬしのみこと</ruby> の足許には、因幡 <ruby>いなば</ruby> の白兎が。
（島根県出雲市・出雲大社）

Unta

KOZO Fujii
Crape myrtle H:62mm
Unta was the popular name given to Izumo Shrine
because it was the biggest brother（Taro）of the three
largest buildings in Japan. Okuninushi, the deity of this
shrine, sits atop the huge pillars of the old building.
（Izumo Taisha, Izumo City, Shimane Pref.）

十二支

平賀明玉斎

象牙　幅40mm

十二支の動物たちが午を中心に
ひとかたまりに彫られています。
馬の背中にいるネズミに比べ、鼻先にいる
蛇が小さいのは、作者が蛇嫌いだから？
（松江市・休憩地）

Twelve Zodiac Animals

MEIGYOKUSAI Hiraga

Ivory　W:40mm

The horse is in the center of this set of
zodiac animals, with a miniscule snake
positioned near its face. A famous design
by this artist, who perhaps disliked snakes!
(Matsue City, Shimane Pref.)

ひと休み

森田正行
黄楊　幅45mm
じゃが芋の上でひと休みしている
2匹のネズミ。中にも1匹。
だれもこないと安心していると、
見つかってしまうかもしれませんよ。
（東京・赤坂御用地内）

Taking a Break

MASAYUKI Morita
Boxwood　W:45mm
Three（!）mice have eaten to their heart's
content. Watch out! Someone is going to
be very unhappy to find that you ate
their potato!
（Akasaka Palace gardens, Tokyo）

初雪

宍戸濤雲
象牙
長30mm
今年の初雪は早いなあ。
せっかくの柿の実が
雪に埋もれてしまいそう。
（東京・赤坂御用地内）

The First Snow

TOUN Shishido
Ivory L:30mm
This year's first snow has come early and
the ripe persimmon fruit is buried under
the snow! The netsuke snow and the real
snow blend into each other in this picture.
(Akasaka Palace gardens, Tokyo)

見にくいアヒルの子

高木喜峰

琥珀　長42mm

琥珀で作った白鳥の子。
白鳥の中に小さな白鳥の
隠れているのが透けて見えます。
琥珀で作られているから
コハクチョウ。
「醜いアヒルの子」と
見にくいアヒルの子。
（島根県・宍道湖畔）

An Ugly Duckling?

KIHO Takagi

Amber L:42mm

Hiding within this amber swan,
there is a baby swan, although
you cannot see it well from any one
angle—a clever rendition of
the *Ugly Duckling* story.
(By Lake Shinji, Shimane Pref.)

北の仲間

高木喜峰
トナカイの角　幅45mm
北極を代表するイッカクと
シロイルカと、ホッキョクグマ。
幸せそうに寝ています。イッカクの
牙は根付の下に隠れています。
（高円宮邸）

Arctic Comrades

KIHO Takagi
Caribou antler　W:45mm
Three mammals representing the arctic,
the narwhal, the beluga, and the polar bear,
are deep in slumber. Will environmental
degradation ruin their world?
(Residence, Tokyo)

イルリアック

針谷絹代（陶作 山本篤）
青磁、トナカイ角、蒔絵　径53mm
イルリアックとは、
グリーンランド語で「氷山」のこと。
北極の氷山。南極のペンギン。
両方の空にオーロラが見えています。
（高円宮邸）

Lulie Illuliaq

KINUYO Hariya
（Atsushi Yamamoto : Porcelain）
Porcelain, caribou antler, lacquer *maki-e*　φ:53mm
Illuliaq means "iceberg" in Greenlandic. The artist made this
to commemorate my children's book *Lulie the Iceberg*, in
which Lulie travels from the Arctic to the Antarctic.
（Residence gardens, Tokyo）

ブリザード

向田陽佳
トナカイ角　高50mm
北極圏の移動には犬ゾリが欠かせません。
凍りつくようなブリザードの中でジーッと
雪嵐が止むのを待ち続ける犬。
かわいそうなので陽溜りで撮りました。
（島根県斐川町・出雲キルト美術館）

Blizzard

YOKA Mukaida
Caribou antler　H:50mm
Made for a netsuke evening on an
arctic theme, this depicts a sled dog
with his eyes narrowed and coat
frozen during a blizzard. I placed
him in the sun to thaw him out!
（Izumo Quilt Museum, Hikawa Town,
Shimane Pref.）

そら

高木喜峰
トナカイ角　高63mm
寒暖計を下げ、オーロラを見ている
イヌイットの少女。
環境が変化していることへの
強いメッセージが込められています。
（東京・赤坂御用地内）

Sky

KIHO Takagi
Caribou antler　H:63mm
This Inuit girl, wearing
a thermometer, looks intently
up at the aurora. Her
environment is changing.
Brilliantly carved,
this little girl sends out
a strong message.
（Akasaka Palace gardens, Tokyo）

注：あたため厳禁！

和地一風
トナカイ角
長52mm
Xmasのブッシュ・ドゥ・ノエルの表面には、
北極圏の景色が彫られています。
ケーキも地球もあたためないように！
（東京・赤坂御用地内）

Warning: Keep Chilled!

IPPU Wachi
Caribou antler L:52mm
Made for a netsuke evening on an arctic
theme, the icing on the Christmas log
depicts the aurora, snow, and migrating
caribou. But the cake must be kept chilled!!
(Akasaka Palace gardens, Tokyo)

寒いよー！

S.オシポフ（ウクライナ）

タグアナッツ　高42mm

ひとり寒さに震える子猿。
みんなはどこに行ってしまったのだろう？
子猿のみじめな眼を見ていると、かけよって
抱きしめてやりたい衝動にかられます。

（高円宮邸）

It's Cold!

Sergey OSIPOV（UKR）

Tagua nut　H:42mm

Where is everybody?? Feeling lonely and
cold, the little monkey shivers in the snow.
His eyes look so forlorn that I always want
to pick him up and cuddle him.

（Residence gardens, Tokyo）

白熊

針谷祐之
トナカイ角、蒔絵　高28mm
小さくなってしまった氷に
しがみついているホッキョクグマ。
蒔絵作者が初めて彫刻に挑戦し、
一人で仕上げた作品です。
（高円宮邸）

Polar Bear

MASAYUKI Hariya
Caribou antler, *maki-e*　H:28mm
A polar bear is worried about the ever-
shrinking size of the ice floe. This work is
the lacquer artist's brilliant first attempt at
carving the base material as well!
(Residence gardens, Tokyo)

ワルツ

高木喜峰

象牙　高42mm

ペンギンは一万羽もいる大集団の中でも
お互いの声を聞き分けるといいます。
ペンギンのカップルが氷の上で
ハートのワルツを楽しんでいます。

（島根県斐川町・出雲キルト美術館）

Waltz

KIHO Takagi

Ivory　H:42mm

During the breeding season, penguins gather
in huge colonies. How do they distinguish
their partners?? This couple decide to dance
a heart-shaped waltz.

（Izumo Quilt Museum, Hikawa Town, Shimane Pref.）

ハニー・ポッサム

升元　一
黄楊　長43mm
ハニー・ポッサムは、
体長4cm、体重10gほどの
かわいい哺乳類。
ほぼ原寸大で作られています。
（高円宮邸）

Honey Possum

KAZU Masumoto
Boxwood　L:43mm
This artist has been carving the various
rare and endangered animals around the
world. This honey possum is only 4cm
long and weighs 10g—netsuke size!
(Residence, Tokyo)

オーロラ

高木喜峰

イッカク牙、琥珀、黒蝶貝　幅53mm

イッカクの牙の根元を利用して
厳しい寒さのなかにもほのぼのとした
温もりを感じる北極の風景を表現しました。
裏面に描いた絵は「氷山のイッカク」。
（高円宮邸）

Aurora

KIHO Takagi

Narwhal tusk, amber, shell　W:53mm

The artist has fitted an abalone shell and
a piece of clear amber into the hollow section
of the narwhal tusk. There is a warmth to
this netsuke, despite the cold arctic setting.
(Residence, Tokyo)

鳥の歌

阿部裕幸

象牙　高48mm

鳩は、時を告げるのもひと苦労。
陰でいつも歌の練習に励んでいるのです。
このような作者の発想に思いを馳せながら
作品を眺めるのも、根付の楽しみ方のひとつ。
（高円宮邸）

The Singing Bird

YUKO Abe

Ivory　H:48mm

From the front, the bird is on duty
and announces the time, but around
the back, the artist shows the bird
hard at work, practicing his singing!
(Residence, Tokyo)

獏家族 ばくかぞく

藤井安剛

鹿角

長125mm

悪夢を食べる獏。

獏のカールした毛が

紐通しの穴となり、

小さな子どもを包み込んでいます。

片面ずつに父獏と

母獏の顔が描かれています。

（島根県斐川町・松園）

A Baku *Family*

ANGO Fujii

Stag antler L:125mm

The *baku* is an imaginary
animal that eats bad
dreams. One side is
the father, the other is the
mother, and a tiny baby
baku can be seen amid
the swirls.

(Shoen, Hikawa Town,
Shimane Pref.)

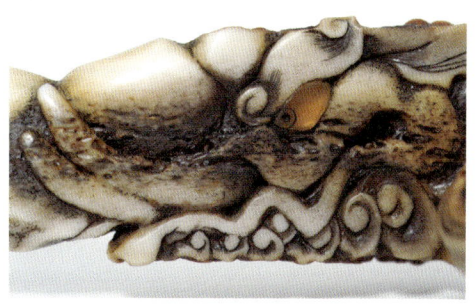

竜

佐々木泰宏

鹿角

幅40mm

玉を手にして、眼を見開いている竜。

怖いはずの竜が、なぜか滑稽に見えます。

八幡垣睦子氏の作品「流転」を背景に撮影。

（島根県斐川町・出雲キルト美術館）

Dragon

YASUHIRO Sasaki

Stag antler　W:40mm

A gentle-looking dragon, he is
portrayed in a flat, circular shape.
From the top, all that is showing is
his head. On the back is carved
a claw holding a golden ball.

（Hikawa Town, Shimane Pref.）

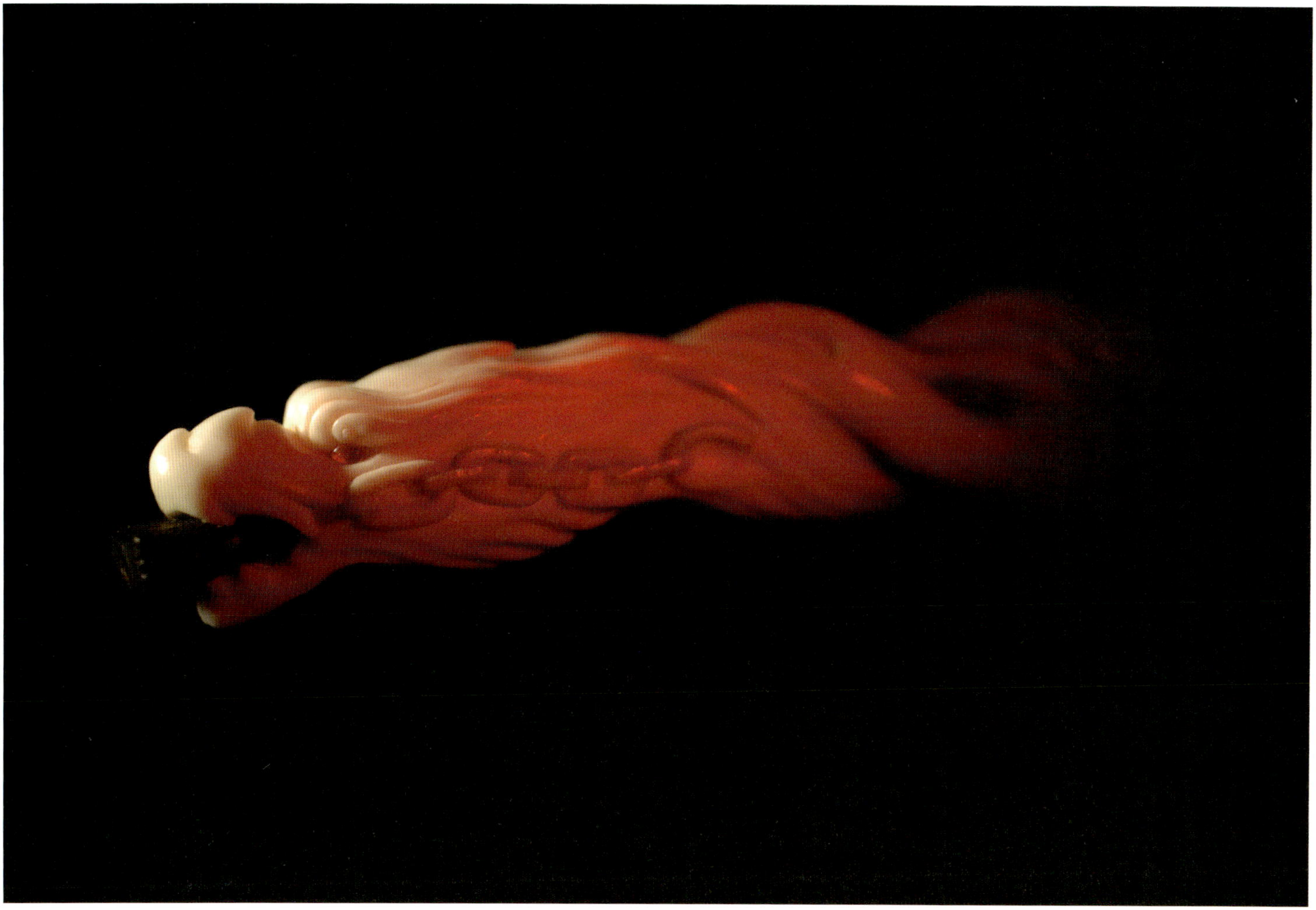

魂の叫び

和地一風

鹿角　長140mm

自己を解放したいという思いが炎となり、
龍に姿を変えて己を縛る鎖を引きちぎる。
龍が口にくわえているのは食いちぎった錠。
紐通しは、作品中央部にあります。

（東京・赤坂御用地内）

The Screaming Soul

IPPU Wachi

Stag antler　L:140mm

There are times when something inside
us can take it no longer. Then the
screaming soul snaps the chains that tie
it down and flies forward, seeking release.

（Akasaka Palace gardens, Tokyo）

献身 けんしん

高木喜峰

鹿角　高66mm

飢えた老人に与える
食べ物となるために、
兎が燃え盛る火に自ら飛び込み、
仏になった、という
仏教説話を題材にした作品です。

（島根県・宍道湖畔）

Sacrifice

KIHO Takagi

Stag antler　H:66mm

This comes from a story in the
Buddhist Jataka tales that says
that all the animals went to
search for food for an old man,
but the rabbit could not find
anything, so he jumped into
the fire and gave himself.
A sad story—but the rabbit
later became the Buddha!

(By Lake Shinji, Shimane Pref.)

睨 にらみ

鈴木裕貴
黄楊　高44mm
刀を手に睨みを利かせている武士。その眼差しの
向けられている先は……。背景の刀は、
江戸時代の刀工津田越前守助廣の作。
日本美術刀剣保存協会にて。
（東京都渋谷区）

Cold Stare

YUKI Suzuki
Boxwood　H:44mm
Keen to photograph this beautifully carved samurai with
an appropriate sword, I asked the Society for Preservation
of the Japanese Art Swords for permission and advice. The
sword shown here by Tsuda Echizen-no-Kami Sukehiro
dates from the Edo Period. (Shibuya Ward, Tokyo)

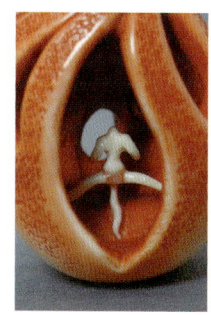

祈り火
和地一風
象牙　高38mm
両手で包み込むような形をした炎。
炎の中に弓矢がつがえられ、
矢の先には鳩が。
鳩は、平和に向かって飛び立ちます。
（島根県奥出雲町・奥出雲たたらと刀剣館）

Praying Flame
IPPU Wachi
Ivory　H:38mm
The flame from hands brought together in prayer.
Inside is a bow and arrow with a dove.
We all pray for world peace.
Photographed on the metal used to make swords.
(Okuizumo Tatara Sword Museum, Okuizumo Town, Shimane Pref.)

根付の歴史と国際化

　根付は帯から何かを下げるときの滑り止です。着物にポケットがなかったために生まれたのかもしれません。はっきりした記録は残っておりませんがその起源は古く、当初は木の根や枝、瓢箪などの自然のものをそのまま適当な大きさに切って使っていたと思われます。江戸時代に、薬や朱肉を入れる印籠、銭金を入れる巾着、煙草入れなどが普及するに従って、いろいろな根付が作られるようになりました。根付は実用品として生まれ、鎖国下の江戸時代で美術工芸品として完成された日本人の感性の結晶です。

　明治期に、西洋文化が導入されると根付の実用性はなくなりますが、日本を訪れた欧米人が根付に興味をもったため、大量に輸出されるようになります。そして根付師は、海外の蒐集家の注文に応ずるべく、伝統的な図柄だけではなく、斬新な形の根付を作るようになります。これらを「現代根付」と呼んでいます。

　根付には、帯から何かを下げるという用途に応じた制約があります。まず、紐を通す穴、または隙間が必要です。これを「紐通し」と呼びます。

　次に、提げ物の装着方法として、根付を帯の内側から通して帯の上部に留める方法と、細長く平らな根付を帯の上から差して留める方法（差し根付）があります。また、数は少ないですが帯を上下から挟む「帯挟み根付」があります。「差し根付」は、小刀の柄から袋を下げて差していた形からの変化で、様式としては古い形です。差し根付は、長くて平らな扁平状をしており、帯の内側から装着する他の根付と違って、帯の上から差し込むため、紐は帯びの外側に見えている状態になります。

　根付には、本来、素材や技法に対する制限は何もありません。まず、素材としては木が一般的で、なかでも黄楊がもっとも多く用いられ、ほかに黒檀、紫檀、桜、胡桃の実などが使用されています。木以外では、象牙、鹿角、猪牙、鯨のひげ、海松、琥珀、陶器などが用いられます。その中で特に象牙はデザインを優先できるといった点で扱いやすい素材です。しかし、今は輸出入禁止の素材も多くあります。多くの素材は色味、質感、形状などを上手に活かしながら題材を表現することになり、作家の想像力と力量が問われます。ただ、蒐集家の観点から申しますと、世界に一点しか存在しない作品となるため、魅力的です。鹿角の根元の不規則な形状や黒檀の色の違い、琥珀に含まれている虫や葉っぱなどをじょうずに構図の中に取り込んだ根付に出会うことは、とても嬉しいものです。

　根付にはいくつかの技法があります。もっとも一般的なのが「形彫根付」（かたぼり）で、人物や動物、鳥類、景色などを立体的に彫ったものです。浮き彫り、半肉彫り（はんにく）、片切り彫り、象嵌などのさまざまな彫刻技法を活かして作り、中を彫り出したものは「穴彫根付」と

呼んでいます。饅頭のように円形で平べったい根付を「饅頭根付」といい、轆轤で作った円い原型に彫りを施したものです。饅頭根付を透かし彫りにしたものを「柳左根付」、象牙や木で円形の台を彫って、その中に金属板の蓋を嵌め込んだものを「鏡蓋根付」といいます。この蓋の部分には刀の鍔や目貫を作る刀装の職人が主にあたりました。能面、神楽面、七福神などをかたどった「面根付」は半立体なので、制作が比較的容易であり、古くから量産されていました。最後に「からくり根付」があります。桃が割れて中に仙人がいたり、栗の中から虫が出てきたりと、内部に意表をつくような細工が隠されている根付です。

　根付を通して日本に興味をもった外国人は大勢おり、海外では学者やコレクターの間で根付の研究が真剣に行われております。現在では、根付のことを調べるのにドイツ語やフランス語の文献を使うことも多々あります。そのようななかで根付は真の国際化を遂げていきます。外国人根付作家の誕生です。今日、海外において根付を制作する者が五十名ほどいるとも聞き、それぞれが強い情熱と向上心をもって制作に励んでいます。もはや根付は日本という伝統を乗り越えて、世界の根付になりつつあるのです。一方、作家たちが世界各地でそれぞれに制作活動をしていることによって、従来とは異なった根付も存在するようになってきました。それは「日本根付」とは異なる「西洋根付」とでもいう

べきものかもしれません。

　元来、西洋美術の基礎が"写実"にあるとするなら、日本美術は"感性"にあると言えるのではないでしょうか。根付彫刻は、着用するという実用性が求められるため、"写実"だけでは通用しません。それでは小さな彫刻作品です。対象をそのまま正確に写し取っても根付という実用にはならないからです。実用的であるためにはできるだけ小さく、丸くなければならないのです。その点、日本人の"感性"をもってすれば、対象をデフォルメして丸く表現しても自然に見えます。

　外国の作家、そして日本の現代作家にも、古典を徹底的に学ぶことと実用目的を果たせる根付の制作を心がけて欲しいと思っています。

　根付の魅力には、その陽気さ、いかに活き活きとしているかがあげられます。日常的に着用されていた時代と違い、以前のように手のひらにとって愛でる機会はありません。根付の写真撮影を始めてから、レンズを通して見ると、彼らが注目されるのを楽しんでいるように見えてなりません。どうやら彼らに、陽気に、活き活きとしてもらうためにどうすればいいか、私なりの解決策を見つけたような気がいたします。

　今後もいろいろな方のお世話になりながら、根付の撮影を続けていきたいと思っております。

History of Netsuke and Their Internationalization

Netsuke are toggles for holding containers and other dangling objects, or *sagemono*, at the *obi*, and the origins date so far back that there is no clear record. Originally, they were natural objects such as roots and dried gourds. With the popularity in the Edo Period (1603-1868) of different types of *sagemono*—from medicine cases to tobacco pouches—came the Golden Age of netsuke. Born purely for practical use, netsuke epitomize the artistic craftsmanship and æsthetic sense of the Japanese during this period.

With the change to Western-style dress during the Meiji Era (1868-1912), netsuke became redundant, but caught the attention of the many foreigners that visited Japan. Huge quantities of netsuke were exported. As time went by, some collectors asked for netsuke that reflected the twentieth century as opposed to purely traditional designs. This was the beginning of "contemporary netsuke."

The restriction in making netsuke relate to its use as a toggle to hold *sagemono* (dangling containers or objects) in place. For this purpose, there must be a cord hole, or *himotoshi*, natural or otherwise, in order to allow a cord to pass through.

There are two ways of attaching the netsuke and *sagemono* to the *obi*, or sash, around the waist. Either the netsuke goes behind the obi and is brought out at the top, or a long netsuke is inserted into the *obi* from the top. The latter type of netsuke is called "*sashi*-netsuke," and these are distinguishable in that they are always long and preferably flat!

There are essentially no restrictions on what materials or techniques are employed. Wood is a popular material, boxwood being the most commonly used. Other woods include ebony, rosewood, and cherry. Walnuts were also used. Other popular materials include ivory, stag antler, boar tusk, baleen, *umimatsu* (black coral), amber, and ceramics. Today, there are export and import restrictions on some materials, including ivory. Artists were able to carve ivory according to whatever design they envisaged, but other materials require imagination and many hours of looking at the materials. The irregular shape of the stag antler, the dark and light tones of different woods, and the various inclusions in the amber result in unique netsuke when their characteristics are cleverly incorporated into the design.

There are several forms of netsuke. The most common is called "*katabori*-netsuke," in which the theme is sculpted "in-the-round." Relief carving, inlay, and other techniques may be used to enhance the resultant three-dimensional netsuke. When carving is done to hollow out the centre, it is called "*anabori*-netsuke." The elongated and flat form, "*sashi*-netsuke," is used when inserting the netsuke into the *obi* from above, and, less commonly, it is made in the "*obi-hasami*" form, in which the netsuke grips the *obi* from both above and below. The "*manju*-netsuke" is round and flat, in the shape of a Japanese cake or bun. A turning lathe is used to make the original shape, and the surface is then carved. When the original shape is kept but is worked so that it looks like lace or latticework, then it is called "*ryusa*-netsuke," and when there is a metal lid on a shallow bowl, it is called "*kagamibuta*-netsuke." Comparatively easy to produce were the masks or "*men*-netsuke," and these exist in large numbers. Popular, but rarer were the "*karakuri*-netsuke." These trick netsuke hide wonderful surprises — from peaches that split open to show sages, to worms that peep out from chestnuts.

For some people, scattered throughout the world, it was netsuke that introduced them to Japan and its culture. There are many scholars and collectors who have done serious research and published books and articles on various aspects of the subject. In that climate of international interest, we saw the birth of foreign netsuke artists. Now numbering around fifty, they are committed and enthusiastic, posing a challenge to any Japanese artist who may be content to believe that making netsuke is a prerogative of their culture. One worry is that the wide-ranging global spread of the artists might divide contemporary netsuke into "Western netsuke" and "Japanese netsuke." Given that Western art has its origins in "realism," there is a tendency to depict something as closely as possible to its true form. Because of its utilitarian purpose, netsuke must be made to be small and round, and pure "realism" cannot be pursued. There is an æsthetic quality that is very important in netsuke. It is my belief that both Japanese and non-Japanese contemporary artists would do well to learn from antique netsuke and to never forget the one important thing that distinguishes a netsuke from any other sculpture — its utilitarian function.

One of the most attractive qualities of netsuke is their liveliness. In order to maintain this, they need to be held and caressed. Because we no longer wear them, it is up to us to find different ways of doing this. It is a great joy for me to have discovered through my camera lens that the netsuke being photographed seemed to be enjoying the attention. There are as many ways of enjoying netsuke as there are collectors, but for the moment, I think that I have discovered a happy solution.

根付作家一覧　List of Artists

外国人作者　　作家名（姓のアルファベット順）／生没年／作品名／収録ページ数の順

参考文献

『根付の研究』
上田令吉著 恒文社 1961年
Ueda, Reikichi. *The Netsuke Handbook*
(Tokyo: Charles E. Tuttle Company, 1978).

『根付 郷コレクション 東京国立博物館蔵』
荒川浩和 講談社インターナショナル 1983年
Arakawa. Hirokazu. *The Go Collection of Netsuke:*
The Tokyo National Museum
(Tokyo: Kodansha International, 1983).

Bushell, Raymond. *Collectors' Netsuke.*
(Tokyo: John Weatherhill, Inc., 1971).

Drosse, Christine. *The Raymond and Frances Bushell*
Collection of Netsuke: A Legacy at the Los Angeles County
Museum of Art
(Chicago: Art Media Resources, 2003).

Lazarnick, George, ed. *MCI: The Meinertzhagen Card*
Index on Netsuke in the Archives of the British Museum,
Part A, B
(New York, Alan R. Liss, Inc., 1986).

Hurtig, Bernard, comp. *Masterpieces of Netsuke Art:*
One Thousand Favorites of Leading Collectors
(Tokyo: John Weatherhill, Inc., 1973).

Kinsey, Miriam. *Contemporary Netsuke*
(Tokyo: John Weatherhill, Inc., 1977).

Kinsey. Miriam. *Living Masters of Netsuke.*
(Tokyo: Kodansha International, 1984).

根付の見られる美術館・博物館

東京国立博物館
東京都台東区上野公園13-9 TEL.03-3822-1111
9:30〜17:00
Tokyo National Museum
13-6 Ueno Koen, Taito-ku, Tokyo

大阪市立美術館（カザールコレクション）
大阪市天王寺区茶臼山1-82　TEL.06-6771-4874
9:30〜17:00
Osaka Municipal Museum of Art
1-82 Chausuyama, Tennoji-ku, Osaka

東京藝術大学美術館
東京都台東区上野公園12-8　TEL.050-5525-2200
10:00〜17:00
The University Art Museum-Tokyo University of the Arts
12-8 Ueno Koen, Taito-ku, Tokyo

京都清宗根付館
京都市中京区壬生賀陽御所町46-1　TEL.075-802-7000
10:00〜16:00
Kyoto Seishu Netsuke Art Museum
46-1 Mibukayougosho, Nakagyo-ku, Kyoto

感謝を込めて

ここ数年、ハンドバッグに根付を入れて出かけます。
機会があればすぐ撮影開始です。
ネーチャーカメラマンの藤原幸一氏には、
当初から励ましていただき、
今でも技術的なことを細かにご指導いただいております。
この根付の写真を見て「本にまとめませんか?」と
講談社の小出和彦氏と立山富喜子さんが
声をかけてくださいました。
ちょっと恥ずかしいものの、ありがたくお話しをお受けいたしました。
いちばん大変な実際の編集作業には
阿部孝嗣氏と山口至剛デザイン室の皆さんがあたってくださり、
英文の校正は友人のStephen Comee氏に頼みました。
お力添えいただいた多くの皆さまに、
この場をお借りして、深く感謝申し上げます。
根付との旅はまだまだ続きます。
いましばらく皆さまには温かく見守っていただきますよう
お願い申し上げます。

根付を撮影中の著者　Photograph by Koichi Fujiwara

Photograph by Koichi Fujiwara

高円宮妃久子（たかまどのみやひ ひさこ）

鳥取滋治郎・二三子夫妻の第一女子としてご誕生。聖心女子学院に学ばれる。1967年よりご家族で渡英。ケンブリッジ大学ガートン・カレッジにて中国学、考古学、人類学をご専攻。1975年にご卒業。この頃より根付の収集を始められる。ご帰国後は、語学力を活かして翻訳や通訳をされていた。1984年、三笠宮憲仁親王殿下とご結婚、高円宮家が創設される。3人のお子さまに恵まれる。（社）いけばなインターナショナル名誉総裁、日本赤十字社名誉副総裁、バードライフ・インターナショナル名誉総裁、国際弓道連盟名誉総裁のほか、2002年11月、憲仁親王殿下が薨去された後は、日本サッカー協会名誉総裁や日加協会名誉総裁など、殿下が務められていた総裁・名誉総裁を引き継がれている。
著書・編著に『氷山ルリの大航海』（講談社）、『夢の国のちびっこバク』（学習研究社）、『宮様との思い出』（産経新聞社）、『根付 高円宮コレクション II』（思文閣出版）などがある。

H.I.H. Princess Hisako of Takamado

The eldest daughter of Shigejiro Tottori, she attended the Sacred Heart School in Tokyo. She moved to the U.K. with her family in 1967. She graduated the University of Cambridge (Girton College) in 1975, having majored in Chinese studies, archaeology, and anthropology. She began collecting netsuke around this time.

In 1984, she married H.I.H. Prince Norihito, the third son of H.I.H. Prince Mikasa, whereupon he had conveyed upon him the title of Prince Takamado. They have three daughters. His Highness passed away in 2002. Her honorary positions include, among others, Honorary President of BirdLife International, Honorary President of Ikebana International; Honorary Vice-President of the Japanese Red Cross Society; Honorary Chairman of the International Kyudo Federation, Honorary Patron of the Canada-Japan Society and Honorary Patron of the Japan Football Association.

Her books include: *Katie and the Dream-Eater* (Oxford: Oxford University Press, 1997); *Lulie the Iceberg* (New York: Kodansha America, 1998); and *Netsuke: The H.I.H. Prince Takamado Collection II* (Tokyo: Shibunkaku Publishing Co., Ltd., 2006).

旅する根付
高円宮妃現代根付コレクション

2008年10月10日　第1刷発行

著者　　高円宮妃久子
発行者　野間佐和子
発行所　株式会社講談社
　　　　〒112-8001 東京都文京区音羽2-12-21
　　　　電話／編集部：03-3534-0553／
　　　　販売部：03-5395-3622／業務部：03-5395-3615
編集協力　阿部孝嗣
企画協力　藤原幸一
AD　　　山口至剛
デザイン　山口至剛デザイン室（島内泰弘／金岡直樹）
印刷所　日本写真印刷株式会社
製本所　大口製本印刷株式会社

© 2008 H.I.H. Princess Hisako of Takamado, Printed in Japan
定価はカバーに表示してあります。

ISBN978-4-06-215001-9　N.D.C.750　196p　21cm

Have Netsuke, Will Travel
H.I.H. Princess Takamado
Contemporary Netsuke Collection

Publication Date : October 10, 2008

Author : H.I.H. Princess Hisako of Takamado

Publisher : Sawako Noma

Publishing : Kodansha Co., Ltd.

　　　　2-12-21 Otowa Bunkyou-ku Tokyo 〒112-8001

　　　　Phone : +81-3-3944-1295

Editorial collaborator : Takashi Abe

Planning collaborator : Koichi Fujiwara

Art Direction : Shigo Yamaguchi

Design : Yasuhiro Shimauchi, Naoki Kanaoka

Printing : Nissha Printing Co., Ltd.

ISBN978-4-06-215001-9